MW01204263

Published by

Texas Fish & Game
Publishing Company, L.L.C.
2350 North Sam Houston Parkway, Suite 240
Houston, Texas 77032
Phone: 281-227-3001
Fax: 281-227-3002
Website: www.fishgame.com

First Edition

Edited by: Don Zaidle

Foreword by: Lefty Kreh

Photography Credits: Cover, back cover, opening and closing spreads, pattern photographs and chapter lead-in photographs by Greg Berlocher. Photograph of Lefty Kreh by Bernard "Lefty" Kreh.

Graphic Design: Wendy Kipfmiller

Layout: Anna Campbell

Texas Saltwater Classics

FLY PATTERNS FOR THE TEXAS COAST

BY GREG BERLOCHER

FOREWORD BY LEFTY KREH

Contents

Chapter Four • Bendbacks

Chapter Five • Attractor Patterns

Chapter 6 • Drum & Sheepshead Patterns

Chapter 7 • Poppers

Chapter 8 • Sliders & Divers

Chapter 9 • Benthic Worms

Chapter 10 • Jetty & Surf Patterns

Contents

To Sarah Elizabeth and all the wonderful memories

Foreword

BY LEFTY KREH

NO ONE WILL OUT-FISH THE BEST LOCAL ANGLER ON HIS OR her waters. One reason is the local fly-fisherman knows which flies are most effective and when and how to use them.

Texas has enormous saltwater flats, channels and bays. Over the years, a number of fly-fishermen have developed flies uniquely effective in these waters.

Many of them may look vaguely familiar: Clouser Minnows, Dahlberg Diver, Lefty's Deceiver, etc., but local fly-fishermen have adjusted the patterns for their own special uses. Fortunately, Greg Berlocher has performed a real service for Texans and those who come here with a fly rod. He collected flies from people that he knows fish hard and well, and have developed patterns for their areas. It says something about fly-fishermen that these men and women are willing to share their efforts with Greg, and you.

Greg has written this book so that not only is there a color photo of each pattern, but detailed tying instructions. An added treat is that there are hints and tips on where, when and how to fish each pattern.

If you fish or plan to fish Texas salt waters, even if you don't tie, this book is a wonderful reference that should help you further enjoy the sport and catch more fish.

Bernard "Lefty" Kreh

October 3, 2001
Hunt Valley, Maryland

Introduction

BY GREG BERLOCHER

THE TEXAS COAST STRETCHES OVER 300 MILES FROM THE eastern border with Louisiana to the southern border with Mexico. Along the way, seven major bay systems punctuate the coastline, each with a unique personality and bountiful angling opportunities for fly-fishermen.

Florida offers magnificent fishing venues for the salty angler, but did you know that Texas is home to over 30% of all the sea grass meadows on the entire Gulf of Mexico? Beginning around the middle Texas coast, sea grass is a dominant feature of many of our bays. Lower Laguna Madre offers almost 250 square miles of shallow flats that average less than three feet in depth. In short, a saltwater fly-fisherman's dream.

Interest in saltwater fly-fishing has swelled over the last 10 years. With that interest came new publications, books, fly-fishing clubs, and Internet sites devoted to saltwater fly-fishing. However, most publications and books have focused on the East Coast, Florida, and the Bahamas. There is a lack of printed information on fly-fishing Texas saltwater. Hence, this book.

My initial goal was to provide novice anglers information on productive patterns for the Texas coast. However, as I began collecting flies from different regions, it became apparent that many seasoned Texas anglers would be interested in learning what other fly-fishermen up and down the coast were using.

The focus of the book is on flies developed by Texans specifically for the Texas coast. Many of the flies are unique and have never been seen outside the developer's circle of friends. Others are old standby patterns that have been tweaked a bit. Whether old or new, they all have one thing in common: They work well on the Texas coast.

Like many fly-fishermen, I have dabbled with fly-tying since I was a kid. Back in the early 60s, there weren't too many places to buy fly-tying materials in Houston, therefore the Herter's Catalog was a treasured text in my house. My two older brothers got first dibs. The three of us would pore over the catalog, committing countless patterns to memory, leaving it dog-eared and wrinkled in a matter of weeks. Logging time tying flies was even more challenging than getting my hands on the catalog. Only when my siblings left the house was I able to sit behind the vise and craft deceptions in feather and fur.

When I took up saltwater fly-fishing as an adult, it wasn't long before I got that old itch to tie my own flies. However, the saltwater flies I desired were much different than the small panfish flies I tied as a youth. To bolster my meager knowledge, I bought dozens of fly-tying books. Unfortunately, most offered only a chapter or two on saltwater flies. Some books featured saltwater patterns, but didn't explain how to tie them. Of the few books I found on saltwater flies that included detailed tying instructions, none included the most important piece of information: How, when, and where to fish the pattern properly.

This book is intended to fill that void. It includes a wide range of patterns that can be fished under a variety of conditions. Baitfish, shrimp, and crab patterns are featured as well as sliders, attractor patterns, and spoon flies. In addition to detailed tying instructions, the developers explain the best season to fish the patterns, best type of water (e.g. sand flats, grass beds, etc.) and the most effective stripping techniques.

Many species that swim our bays are great adversaries on a fly rod. Speckled trout, redfish, and flounder are the "Big Three" of the Texas coast, but many other species provide good sport when caught on the fly. Skipjack (a.k.a. ladyfish) always bring a smile to an angler's face as they leap and dance like miniature tarpon. Black drum and sheepshead are often seen feeding on the flats, and coaxing them to bite is quite a challenge. The collection of flies featured in this book will catch just about anything that swims a Texas bay.

The group of featured tiers is an interesting bunch. Many have been fly-fishing since they were kids, and quite a few were saltwater fly-fishing pioneers on the Texas coast. Many began fly-fishing the salt in the 60s and 70s, and one of them got his first taste of saltwater in 1952.

Experience notwithstanding, they all share a common design philosophy: simplicity. In addition to productivity, a pattern has to be quick and easy to tie. The patterns presented here lend themselves to novice tiers and to those with busy schedules. Many of the flies can be completed in a matter of minutes.

The Texas coast is a windy place. It isn't a matter of if it will blow, but how hard. Windless days are as rare as ninety-foot casts and whooping cranes. A fly that casts easily into a stiff breeze is a valuable advantage. With the exception of a few specialty patterns, all of the flies described herein are very easy to cast.

Texas has become a popular winter destination for fly-fishermen from northern states who appreciate our mild temperatures, spectacular grass-lined flats, and warm hospitality. It is my hope that this tome will become a useful aid for travelling anglers as they prepare for a trip to the Lone Star State. Perhaps it will in some small measure recompense the many fellow fly-fishermen in Colorado, Wyoming, Montana, and Idaho who I have asked, "What is a good pattern to use around here?"

If you are new to saltwater fly-fishing or fly-tying, I hope this text provides a foundation on which you can build over the coming years. Regardless of your experience, the learning never stops.

Greg Berlocher

September 2001
Houston, Texas

CHAPTER 1
Shrimp Patterns

Scates' Shrimp

CAPTAIN CHUCK SCATES

MATERIALS

Hook:	Mustad 34007, No. 2-4
Thread:	Size 3/0, color to match body
Antennae:	Marabou, black Bucktail, white
Body:	Chenille, white
Eyes:	Bead chain eyes, plastic
Legs:	Krystal Flash, pearl Hackle, black

LIKE LONE STAR BEER AND THE ALAMO, THE SCATES SHRIMP is uniquely Texan. Featured in several national fly-fishing magazines and produced commercially by several fly merchants, the pattern is a staple for many fly-fishermen along the coast.

Captain Chuck Scates literally wrote the book on fly-fishing the Texas coast. Teaming with nationally-known writer Phil Shook and world-class photographer David Sams, the trio produced *Fly Fishing the Texas Coast: Backcountry Flats to Blue Water*. The text is a must-read for any serious coastal fly-fisherman.

Scates began tying flies about the same time he started guiding fly-fishermen in 1989. "I wanted a shrimp pattern that was more realistic in the water, and also something that was easy to tie," he said. "Back then, all the shrimp patterns were either very involved to tie, or had epoxy bodies."

Scates noted that pink, white, and brown shrimp all migrate to the Gulf to spawn. The immature shrimp start showing up in the bays during the spring, pushed by high spring tides and strong winds from the south. Therefore, Scates does not use the pattern as much during the winter, waiting until shrimp are more abundant in the bays.

Scates explained that grass shrimp, a completely different species than the penaeid shrimp mentioned above, live their whole lives in the bays. "For some reason, trout tend to regurgitate more in the winter time than during the summer," he said. "Some days the trout will spit out lots of grass shrimp, giving us a clue when to fish the pattern during the winter."

The Scates Shrimp is a good choice for sight-casting or blind-casting. For sight-casting to stationary trout and redfish in skinny water, Scates likes to throw an unweighted fly. The palmered hackle allows a quiet presentation.

When fish are holding in two-foot depths, he prefers a fly with bead chain eyes to get it down into the strike zone quickly.

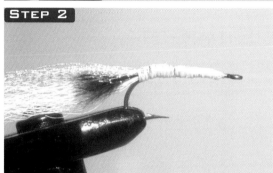

On overcast or foggy days, when sight-casting is out of the question, many fly-fishermen resort to blind-casting the edges of channels or guts. For this specialized duty, Scates suggested adding two sets of bead chain eyes when fish are suspended 3-4 feet down.

Scates strips his namesake shrimp a number of different ways, letting the fish dictate the best retrieve. "Shrimp don't just naturally wait for a predator to come up and eat them," he noted. "They do their best to escape." He likes to strip the fly quickly to imitate a fleeing shrimp, but cautioned against stripping so fast that fish loose sight of it.

TYING INSTRUCTIONS

STEP 1 Tie in bucktail down shank to build up body. Bucktail extends 2 hook lengths past bend. Add marabou stems at bend.

STEP 2 Tie in 15-20 2- to 3-inch strands Krystal Flash along shank.

STEP 3 Tie in chenille near eye, lay on shank, wind thread back over it. Tie in eyes.

STEP 4 Figure-8 wrap chenille up and around eyes. Tie hackle ahead of chenille. Wrap chenille to eye, tie off. Do not cut thread.

STEP 5 Wind hackle around body to eye, tie off. Do not cut thread. Clip standing hackle off back.

STEP 6 Stretch flash over clipped hackle, hold bundle in place with several tight wraps near eye. Pull loose flash down on either side of eye, secure with additional wraps. Trim flash even with hackle legs.

VARIATIONS

The Scates' Shrimp can be tied in numerous color combinations including white, pink, black, brown and green. Choose a contrasting color for the hackle body. One or two pairs of metal bead chain eyes can be added for fishing in deeper water. Captain Scates suggested adding a weedguard if using metal eyes.

Baffin Mud Bug

CAPTAIN PALMER SIMPSON

MATERIALS

Hook:	Mustad 34007, No. 4
Thread:	Ultra Thread 140; color white
Weedguard:	40-pound mono
Antennae:	Flashabou dubbing, copper Stripped, dyed hackle quills
Mouth:	Antron Body-Wool, fluorescent white
Forelegs:	Krystal Flash, clear
Eyes:	Dazl Eyes, 1/8-inch, gold
Tail:	White grizzly hackles
Body:	Medium Ice Chenille, clear
Head:	White grizzly hackle

BAFFIN BAY IS AN INTERESTING BODY OF WATER. BORDERED BY the legendary King and Kennedy Ranches, Baffin is well known for the petrified worm casings that lay hidden beneath its surface. Neophyte boaters have lost many a lower unit to the "rocks" in the bay.

Baffin is also one of the few hypersaline bodies of water in the world. While normal seawater has a salt content of 30 parts per thousand (PPT), Baffin routinely runs over 40 PPT and occasionally up to 75 PPT. The high salinity is exacerbated during the dry summer months and prolonged periods of drought.

"We don't have a normal shrimp population here in Baffin," said Captain Palmer Simpson of Riviera. "Shrimp are in the bay during the spring; however, they disappear when the salinity level goes up in the summer. If we get some good rains later in the year, they tend to stay a while longer.

"The shrimp that you do see in Baffin Bay are normally quite large. Since we don't have lots of little grass shrimp, I needed a larger shrimp pattern. That was why I developed the Baffin Mudbug. I chose that name because our shrimp head up into the creeks when the salinity level gets too high in the bay and bury themselves in the mud.

"My goal was to create a pattern that was easy to cast but had a large profile. I chose the Flashabou dubbing because it created the illusion of size, while being extremely light. Plus, it has a lot of sparkle, which I think is essential in a successful pattern."

Simpson fishes the Baffin Mudbug only during spring. When the salinity level rises, he switches to baitfish or crab imitations. His favorite sight-casting locations include tidal lakes and shorelines with hard sand bottoms, over sandbars, and sand pockets in grass beds.

He prefers a strip-strip-pause retrieve, making 4-5 inch strips. The Baffin Mudbug makes a pretty fair streamer when forced into action. "I have walked up on reds blowing up on finger mullet several times and I didn't have

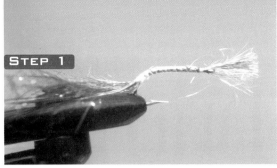

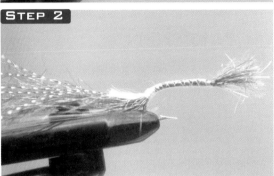

time to change flies," he said. "Cast into the action and buzz it out of there."

TYING INSTRUCTIONS

STEP 1 Tie weedguard behind eye, secure down shank, wrap thread halfway down bend. Wrap thread forward and secure 3-inch bundle Flashabou behind eye. Working backward, secure dubbing to shank. Wrap dubbing around bend to 60 degrees.

STEP 2 Strip 4 hackle quills, secure 2 on either side at 60 degrees. Quills curve outward, not exceeding length of dubbing. Trim excess tags. Tie 4-6 strands Krystal Flash. Combine two ¾-inch lengths wool, secure on bend to extend ½ inch.

STEP 3 Tie 2 hackles on either side, angled down and out 45 degrees, extending 1½ inches from thread wraps. Figure-8 wrap eyes where thread wraps end. Coat wraps with head cement.

STEP 4 Select a webby grizzly hackle, tie in near eyes. Palmer in behind and ahead of eyes with 6-8 turns, tie off.

STEP 5 Cut 6½ -inch piece Ice Chenille, strip ½ inch off one end, secure string to shank just behind eye. Wind chenille back to base of palmered hackle. Make several more chenille wraps to create wide spot in body. Wrap chenille forward, creating tapered body. Tie off weedguard, whip finish. Coat wraps with head cement.

STEP 6 Trim chenille leaving smooth, cigar-like body. Do not trim chenille touching palmered hackle. Trim tail to extend ⅛ inch ahead of eye.

VARIATIONS

Captain Simpson has also had good luck substituting olive hackles and brown Ice Chenille.

Brooks' Shrimp

BROOKS BOULDIN

MATERIALS

Hook:	Mustad 34007 or Tiemco 811S, No. 4
Thread:	3/0 Monocord, White
Weed guard:	18-pound Hard Mason (optional)
Antennae:	Dry fly grade neck hackle, grizzly Dark horsehair from tail or mane
Rostrum:	Bleached deer body hair
Feelers:	Marabou, white
Eyes:	Mono nymph eyes
Carapace:	Swiss straw, white
Legs:	Crystal Chenille, white
Body:	SealX, creamy white

BROOKS BOULDIN HAS DEVOTED MANY YEARS OF HIS LIFE to fly-fishing. Founder and owner of Angler's Edge in Houston from 1986 until 2001, he finally retired to spend more time on the water. Over the years, he developed several innovative saltwater patterns.

Bouldin developed Brooks' Shrimp back in the 1980s "out of necessity."

"At the time, there weren't any good shrimp patterns available for use on the Texas coast," he told me.

Having taught beginning and advanced fly-tying for many years, Bouldin concluded there are four major factors common to all good saltwater patterns. First, a fly must have good movement in the water. Bouldin is a big fan of marabou and chose it for the antennae on this pattern. When stripped, the fly really exhibits a lot of action.

Second, a fly must provide a good silhouette in the water. Bouldin noted that the suggestion of the shrimp's carapace was very important, but an exact imitation is not required.

Third, the size and color of the pattern need to be right for the situation. Throughout the year, there will be white, pink, and brown shrimp in a variety of sizes in our bays.

Lastly, the sink rate needs to be appropriate for the depth. Bouldin noted that many flies are weighted too heavily and sink rapidly to the bottom. This is problematic if there are only six inches of water on top of a thick grass bed. "I prefer flies that will linger in the strike zone before sinking," Bouldin said. "When fishing in deeper water, I simply count the fly down before beginning my retrieve."

When sight-casting in shallow water, Bouldin likes to fish his shrimp pattern with snappy 6-8 inch strips. "A fleeing shrimp isn't going to dawdle once it is seen," he said. "It will try desperately to escape."

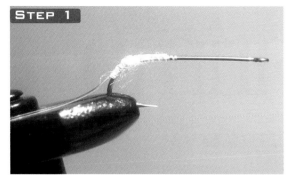

STEP 1

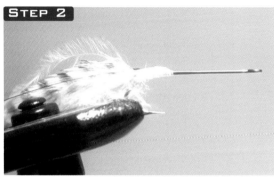

STEP 2

STEP 3

STEP 4

STEP 5

Bouldin was also quick to point out that you should change your stripping technique if the fish do not cooperate. "If you get refusals with 6-8 inch strips, vary your retrieve until you find something appealing to the fish."

TYING INSTRUCTIONS

STEP 1 Tie in weedguard at bend. Add small amount of dubbing to thread, form small knot on bend above barb.

STEP 2 Tie in horsehair antennae at knot so they flare a bit. Create rostrum by clipping small bundle of bleached hair, evening tips and tying immediately ahead of knot. Hair should flare slightly. Add 6-8 plumes white marabou.

STEP 3 Figure-8 wrap eyes atop other materials. Tie in 4-inch segment of Swiss Straw behind eyes. Swiss Straw should extend behind bend. Add short segment Crystal Chenille behind eyes, extending behind bend.

STEP 4 Form 8-inch dubbing loop, coat lightly with dubbing wax, add SealX, tighten with spinning tool. (Dubbing loop not shown.) Figure-8 wrap dubbing in and around eyes, forming thorax. Use remaining dubbing to form evenly tapered body. Thorax should cover ⅓ of shank, body ⅔.

STEP 5 Figure-8 length of thorax with chenille. Trim chenille atop thorax, pull Swiss Straw across thorax; make several thread wraps to hold in place where thorax meets body. Pull Swiss Straw over body and overwrap with thread to eye. Space overwraps to form segmented body. Trim Swiss Straw, leaving ¼ inch extending beyond eye. Split overhanging Swiss Straw, forming V-shaped tail. Tie off loose end of weed guard, whip finish. Use bodkin to tease out a few fibers from dubbed body, enhancing chenille legs.

VARIATIONS

Brooks' Shrimp can be tied in brown, chartreuse, olive, or pink.

Cactus Shrimp

JOE A. DEFORKE

MATERIALS:

Hook:	Mustad 34007, No. 2, 4 or 6
Thread:	3/0, black
Weedguard:	15-pound Hard Mason (optional)
Eyes:	Bead chain (optional)
Tail:	Fox squirrel, calf tail, bucktail or marabou
Body:	Cactus Chenille, size small
Wing:	Fox squirrel, calf tail, bucktail or marabou

JOE DEFORKE IS THE ARCHETYPE TEXAS ANGLER THAT started fly-fishing the Texas coast over the last decade. An avid fisherman his entire life, he spent countless hours prospecting for trout and reds with a levelwind reel.

Then in the mid-1980's, DeForke noticed that he and his friends were catching fewer fish on their outings. It was then that he took up fly-fishing. "I was looking to have more fun while on the water," he told me.

With no fly-fishing background to draw from, DeForke ordered his first fly rod from the Cabela's catalog. In his quest for knowledge, he discovered Houston-based Texas Fly Fishers, the largest fly-fishing club in the state. New friends eagerly shared their knowledge of fishing the salt, and shortly thereafter DeForke started tying his own flies.

"It was almost an accident how I developed the Cactus Shrimp," he said. "I came across a package of Crystal Chenille, which was brand new at the time, and wondered if I could come up with some sort of pattern with it."

The Cactus Shrimp is a slow-sinking bendback pattern that is ideal for trout and redfish. Over the years, DeForke has caught many other species on the fly, including croaker, whiting, flounder, black drum, and even a few piggy perch and hardhead catfish. "The Cactus Shrimp seems to appeal to just everything in the bay," DeForke said.

He explained that normally he fishes an unweighted Cactus Shrimp, but sometimes adds bead chain eyes to make it sink faster. He cautioned that the fly will foul in grass beds if allowed to settle.

DeForke lets his prey dictate how he fishes the pattern. He typically casts directly at tailing or cruising fish, and retrieves with 4- to 6-inch strips. If the fish are lethargic, he adjusts to 3- to 4-inch strips with frequent pauses. If fish charge the fly, a fast retrieve triggers strikes.

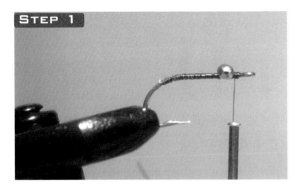

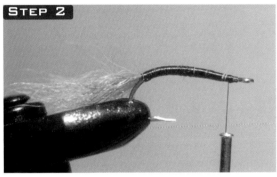

TYING INSTRUCTIONS

STEP 1 De-barb and sharpen hook. Wrap eye-to-bend thread base, coat with cement. Tie in weedguard (optional) and eyes (optional). Place eyes two hook-eye widths back atop shank.

STEP 2 Tie in calf or marabou tail. If calftail, split into two bundles, tie on either side of hook. Tie tail on bend so it points slightly up. Add head cement.

STEP 3 Tie in cactus chenille near bend, wrap thread forward to eye. Wrap chenille on shank, tie off near eye. Add head cement.

STEP 4 Tie in squirrel wing; substitute calf- or bucktail. Whip finish, coat thread wraps with head cement. Add head cement to the lower ⅓ of wing to stiffen.

VARIATIONS

DeForke ties the Cactus Shrimp in a number of variations. Color choices include, white, pink, root beer, brown, black, orange, and chartreuse. You can tie the Cactus Shrimp in a solid color or add a contrasting wing.

Small hackle feathers can be used in lieu of the squirrel-tail wing, but you should add a weedguard.

DeForke recommended white or pink when fishing under lights, orange or chartreuse when chasing tailing reds, and black or brown when fishing for black drum.

Frito Shrimp

CAPTAIN BILL HAGEN

MATERIALS:

Hook:	Mustad 34007, No. 4
Thread:	Flymaster Plus, tan
Bead:	Brass bead, small
Body:	Kraft Fur, tan Medium Ultra Chenille, dark tan
Flash:	Krystal Flash, black
Eyes:	Burned mono eyes, 32-pound Hard Mason
Weedguard:	15-pound Hard Mason
Glue:	5-minute epoxy
Paint:	Oil based model paint, black

WHEN HE ISN'T PROSECUTING BAD GUYS AS AN ASSISTANT U.S. Attorney in Brownsville, Captain Bill Hagen spends his free time fly-fishing the waters of Lower Laguna Madre. He paroles most of the fish he catches, keeping perhaps one a month for fresh *ceviche.*

An accomplished angler who twice won the South Padre Invitational Fly Fishing Tournament, Hagen also enjoys crafting new saltwater patterns.

Most of his patterns imitate the natural forage he finds in fishes' stomachs. While cleaning his catch, Hagen's post-mortem often reveals the specific species, size, and sometimes color of bait the fish had been feeding on.

"If I open up a fish and it is full of shrimp or crabs, I know which fly to try first on my next trip," he told me. "Chances are, the fish will continue their selective feeding habits for a few days, making it easier to catch them. I find it enjoyable to figure out what will work in a specific situation."

Rarely carrying more than five or six patterns in his fly box, his selections include a mix of crab, baitfish, and shrimp patterns. One of his favorite creations is the Frito Shrimp. The pattern acquired its unusual moniker when one of his fly-fishing clients came close to eating a fly that had accidentally fallen into a bag of Fritos® Corn Chips. The name stuck.

Unlike the pink, white, and brown shrimp (collectively known as "penaeid shrimp") that inhabit our bays, grass shrimp are actually a different species. Most of these crustaceans are tiny, and come in a variety of hues.

The Frito Shrimp's small size makes it ideal when casting in a foot or less of water; a quiet entry is essential when fishing skinny water. The fly's compactness also makes it is easy to cast, a definite plus when coastal breezes kick up.

Hagen recommended short, snappy strips no longer than 4 inches when fishing this pattern. "The shrimp

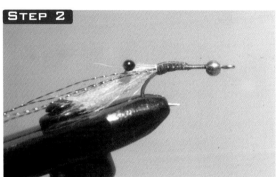

you are imitating are quite small, and the action you impart must mimic the real thing," he said.

TYING INSTRUCTIONS

STEP 1 Place bead on hook. Tie in small tuft Kraft Fur atop shank, length 2 times hook. Add Krystal Flash antennae.

STEP 2 Burn tips of mono, coat with epoxy tinted with black paint. Rotate eyes until dry. Tie in eyes mid-shank to extend ¼ inch past end of hook. Splay eyes outward.

STEP 3 Dub thick part of body with Kraft Fur, extending 1 wrap beyond base of eyes.

STEP 4 Slide bead against eye. Tie in Ultra Chenille ahead of dubbed material, wrap back to bead. Tie off and clip chenille.

STEP 5 Trim body to shape. Add weedguard and tie off.

VARIATIONS

The Frito Shrimp can be tied in many different colors. Tan, light brown, dark brown, green, and olive are good options. For a more durable fly, Captain Hagen suggested working some Flexament into the clipped body. A weedguard is optional, but recommended for fishing over shallow grass.

Jim's Matagorda Pistol Shrimp

JIM GREEN

MATERIALS:

Hook:	Mustad 34007, No. 2-4
Thread:	6/0 Uni, rust brown
Weedguard:	30-pound Climax hard mono
Tail:	Red fox squirrel tail, Rootbeer Krytal Flash, Sili Legs, pumpkin, green orange
Eyes:	Large bead chain, black
Body:	Chenille, brown pearl tinsel Chenille, tan

LIKE MANY OF THE FEATURED FLY-TIERS IN THIS BOOK, JIM Green has spent many years mastering the art of catching fish on flies. In addition to 40 years of fly-fishing experience, he also brings scientific credentials to the tying bench. A former biologist for the U.S. Fish and Wildlife Service, Green is keenly aware of the different marine organisms that inhabit our bays.

The genesis of this pattern was when a fellow biologist doing a gut study on red drum found a fish filled with a mixture of half crab and half pistol shrimp. "I had never seen a pistol shrimp pattern before, so I decided to create one," Green said.

Pistol shrimp (sometimes called "snapping shrimp") are small crustaceans similar in appearance to crawfish with one large claw, which is used for defense and feeding. They live in and around dead oyster shells. Since live oysters often build on top of dead shell, just about any oyster reef is sure to hold some pistol shrimp.

Pistol shrimp get their name from the pistol-like popping sound they make with their pincher. The sound is audible above the surface and signals their presence to the trained ear. Green suggested filling your kitchen sink full of water and then snapping your fingers under water. The sound of a pistol shrimp is almost identical.

"Shuffle your feet through any old oyster shell and they will give themselves away," he said. "Once you hear them, you can be confident that Jim's Pistol Shrimp will work well in the area."

Most pistol shrimp have a tan or cinnamon abdomen and coppery-red carapace. Green noted that coloration varies a bit from bay to bay in the way crawfish vary between lakes.

Green added that you will not find pistol shrimp on sand or mud bottoms unless there is nearby shell or rock for the crustaceans to hide in. He favors fishing grass flats with scattered shell.

Green fishes the middle Texas coast primarily during the summer, preferring 1-3 feet of water. He suggested using a larger hook and adding more weight to fish the deeper oyster reefs of the upper coast.

The recommended retrieve for this fly is jerky, 4- to 6-inch strips.

TYING INSTRUCTIONS

STEP 1 Tie weedguard on shank, continue wrapping part way down bend. Tie in squirrel tail length of shank to build tail. Tie in several strands Krystal Flash 1 times length of shank, secure with thread wraps. Tie in Sili Legs twice length of hook, secure.

STEP 2 Figure-8 wrap eyes in position shown. Tie in copper chenille, wrap back ⅓ of body, tie off.

STEP 3 Tie in tan chenille, wrap forward covering remaining ⅔ of body. Tie off ¹⁄₁₆ inch behind eye. Tie off weedguard, whip finish.

Petrie Shrimp

MARK PETRIE

MATERIALS:

Hook:	Mustad 34011, No. 2
Thread:	6/0, red
Weedguard:	25-pound Hard Mason
Tail:	Sparkle Yarn Marabou, chartreuse
Antennae:	Rubber bands, small round, black
Body:	Furry Foam
Legs:	Ice Chenille, large
Eyes:	Nylon dumbbell, large

MARK PETRIE IS AN ARTIST BEHIND THE VISE.
Literally. In addition to crafting patterns for his fly box, Mark ties art flies for exhibitions.

Never one to accept the status quo, Petrie is also a prolific developer of new patterns for the salt. Mark puts a new pattern through its paces before taking it to the bay. First, a promising fly gets the dunk test in the kitchen sink. Upon satisfactory results, it is off to the neighbor's pool where Petrie observes the pattern's action when stripped.

"About ten years ago, when Dave Hayward was the manager of Orvis Houston, he asked me to develop a unique shrimp pattern they could sell in their shop," Petrie recalled. "The Petrie Shrimp was the result."

Since the pattern's inception, the Petrie Shrimp has become its creator's confidence fly. "Everything in the bay eats shrimp," he said. Petrie's largest speckled trout caught on the Petrie Shrimp weighed over 6 pounds.

The Petrie Shrimp is a versatile pattern that can be fished in depths from 6 six inches to 4 feet. Although its creator likes to sight-cast to tailing reds, he really likes catching big trout. "Big trout are much easier to catch in 4 feet of water," he said. That being the case, he does quite a bit of blind-casting .

"You can cast the Petrie Shrimp easily with a 6-weight rod," he told me. "I can blind-cast with a lighter rod for several hours without getting tired."

When fishing the Petrie Shrimp in deeper water, Petrie starts with big strips separated by half-second pauses. "If you don't get any bites, by all means change your retrieve until you find something the fish like," he said.

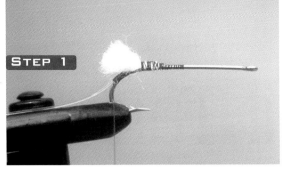

TYING INSTRUCTIONS

STEP 1 Wrap mid-shank-to-bend thread base. Add weedguard, continue wraps past bend. Add 2 short strips Sparkle Yarn atop shank.

STEP 2 Add 1 or 2 shank-length marabou hackles atop Sparkle Yarn. Add antennae atop marabou, extending up 45 degrees.

STEP 3 Trim to a point ⅜-inch strip Furry Foam. Tie point of Furry Foam and 3 inches Ice Chenille to shank atop antennae. Tie in eyes atop chenille.

STEP 4 Wrap Ice Chenille forward ⅛ inch, tie off, trim excess.

STEP 5 Fold Furry Foam over chenille, tie with 7 wraps.

STEP 6 Mentally divide remaining shank into 3 segments, tie Furry Foam at each location. Furry Foam edges should meet neatly below shank, creating round carapace. Trim excess Furry Foam straight across near eye, shape edge into shrimp tail slightly wider than foam-covered shank. Tie off weedguard and trim, whip finish.

Patrick's Tail Tamer

PATRICK ELKINS

MATERIALS:

Hook:	Mustad 34007, No. 4
Thread:	3/0 Flymaster Plus, white or tan
Eyes:	Extra large black mono nymph eyes
Legs:	Tuft of white rabbit hair, cut from a Zonker strip
Antennae:	2 splayed grizzly hackles Black Flashabou
Head:	Tuft of white rabbit hair, cut from a Zonker strip
Body:	Flashabou Minnow Body (Mylar)
Rattle:	Standard glass worm rattle, size medium
Wing:	5-10 strands gold Crystal Flash over tan and white bucktail

PATRICK ELKINS FONDLY RECALLED THE TIME HE SPENT between graduation from college and starting his first job. "I was on the same school of redfish every day for several weeks, but I couldn't get them to eat anything consistently," he said. "They were in 7-10 inches of water, and I must have thrown every fly I owned at them."

Elkins described how the fish ignored Clouser Minnows and Seaducers of all shades and hues. The splat of a small popper would send the bronze battlers on a panicked rush for deeper water. "I had determined that the fish were dining exclusively on shrimp, and suspected that something that sounded like a shrimp would trigger a strike," Elkins said. "That was the inspiration for Patrick's Tail Tamer."

Elkins' parents live on Galveston Island and he has spent enough time on the water to understand the seasonal shrimp migration. "About May each year, immature shrimp migrate from the Gulf into the back marshes of West Galveston Bay," he explained. "The shrimp are only about an inch long, and completely white. Redfish push back into the shallows and gorge on the new shrimp crop."

Elkins prefers smaller versions of the pattern in May, and scales up as the summer progresses. He uses solid white flies early in the season, moving to a tan or light brown color in August.

Patrick's Tail Tamer is also a big hit with redfish in Lower Laguna Madre when tied with a gold Mylar body topped with a light tan over orange wing.

When sight-casting, Elkins throws to a single or group of fish and begins stripping once the fly is in range. "When the tail slides beneath the surface, you are getting ready to get a strike," he said. "This fly really drives the fish nuts."

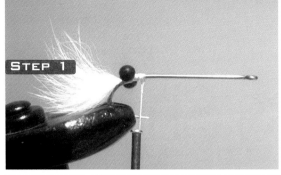
STEP 1

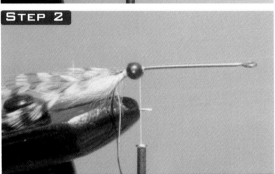
STEP 2

STEP 3

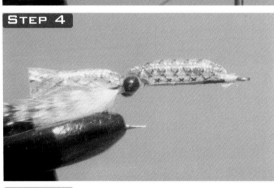
STEP 4

STEP 5

NOT SHOWN

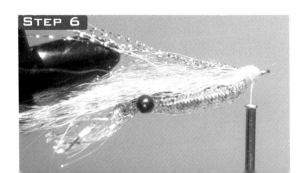
STEP 6

Patrick's Tail Tamer is an excellent choice for blind-casting as well, especially in turbid conditions. The noise helps fish find the pattern in off-colored water. Elkins suggested retrieving the fly slowly with long, slow strips when fishing in sandy water.

TYING INSTRUCTIONS

STEP 1 Wrap mid-shank-to-bend thread base. Tie in eyes and a small tuft rabbit fur ahead of eyes.

STEP 2 Tie in 2 grizzly hackles atop rabbit fur, hackles splayed to either side of fur, extending slightly farther. Tie in 2 long strands black Flashabou atop hackles.

STEP 3 Tie in a 2-inch minnow body atop fur, hackles, and black Flashabou, extending to tip of the rabbit fur in front, to eye in back.

STEP 4 Wind thread, then 2 strands black Flashabou to eye to simulate "vein." Insert rattle into tubing from eye end, and tie off at eye.

STEP 5 (Not shown.) Coat body and eyes with epoxy (30 minutes to 2 hours set time), rotate until dry.

STEP 6 Form wing with 5-10 strands gold Krystal Flash over small bunch tan bucktail over a small bunch white bucktail, extending to end of rabbit fur. Whip finish, cement head.

VARIATIONS

Patrick's Tail Tamer can be tied with copper or gold Flashabou atop an orange-over-tan wing. This combination is especially effective for redfish in Lower Laguna Madre.

East Cut Grass Shrimp

T.J. NEAL

MATERIALS:

Hook:	Mustad 34007, No. 2-6
Thread:	Size A Danville Flymaster Plus, black
Weedguard:	40-lb. mono
Antennae:	Krystal Flash, black Krystal Flash, Chartreuse #2 saddle hackles, chartreuse
Eyes:	50-lb. Mono
Body:	Medium tinsel chenille, chartreuse #2 saddle hackle, chartreuse

T. J. NEAL STARTED FLY-FISHING THE PORT MANSFIELD area with his dad, Captain Terry Neal, at age 10. "While growing up, I never had a reason to tie anything," he said. "If I ever needed flies, I would borrow a few that dad had tied."

Upon graduation from Texas A & M, he went to work full time for Orvis in Austin. It was then that he took up fly-tying. During his tenure in the retail business, he realized there was an unfilled market niche for patterns tailored to the Texas coast. So, the industrious 24-year-old started his own company.

T. J. Neal's flies quickly gained in notoriety and are now sold in fly shops across the state. Some are original patterns, while others are old standards downsized for skinny water.

"Quite a few grass shrimp on the market today are epoxy patterns," Neal told me. "They sink too fast to be fished effectively on shallow flats. Plus, they are stiff and lifeless under water. I wanted a small pattern that would sink very slowly, and I wanted to incorporate feathers so the fly would pulsate in the water."

The result was the East Cut Grass Shrimp. It is a small pattern ideally suited for casting to cruising trout and redfish. Because of its small size, Neal fishes this pattern on a 5-weight outfit when the wind cooperates, and a 7-weight in gustier weather.

Neal said the best way to fish the East Cut Grass Shrimp is to cast 1 1/2 feet in front of a cruising fish. Leading the fish is very important so the fly will have time to sink into the strike zone. Then he employs a smooth, steady retrieve using 4-6 inch strips.

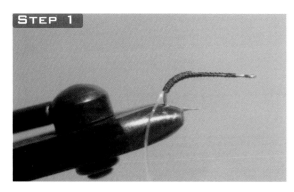

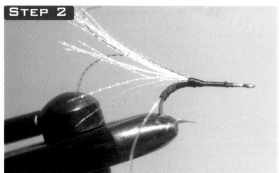

TYING INSTRUCTIONS

STEP 1 Wrap shank to bend as shown, tie in weedguard around bend, leave end loose.

STEP 2 Tie in 10 strands chartreuse Krystal Flash extending 1 hook length beyond bend. Tie in two 4- to 6-inch strands black flash.

STEP 3 Trim 2 matching hackles to extend 1½ inch past bend, tie in on either side of hook.

STEP 4 Tie in eyes even with bend. Tie in hackle ahead of eyes, form collar with 4 wraps around shank. Tie off.

STEP 5 Restart thread near eye, tie in tinsel chenille. Wrap chenille to collar, then to front. Tie off, complete weedguard.

VARIATIONS

The East Cut Grass Shrimp can be tied in a variety of colors, including pink, orange, tan, red, and brown.

CHAPTER 2
Baitfish Patterns

Rob's Zydeco Minnow

CAPTAIN ROBERT WOODRUFF

MATERIALS:

Hook:	Mustad 34011, No. 2
Thread:	Danvilles, flat waxed nylon
Glue:	Zap-A-Gap or Superglue
Rattle:	Excalibur Thunder Rattle
Tail:	Krystal Flash Marabou, white
Body:	EZ Body braided tubing, size large
Eyes:	Bead chain, medium

CAPTAIN ROB WOODRUFF GREW UP FLY-FISHING, WHICH could be due to genetic predisposition. In the 1950s, Rob's dad, using the Herter's Catalog as his sole resource, started crafting patterns using gold crappie hooks and feathers salvaged from hunting trips. Rob demonstrated the mark of a serious sportsman early in life, requesting subscriptions to fishing magazines instead of toys for his sixth birthday.

Although he now guides fly-fishermen on Lake Fork for a living, Woodruff also enjoys trips to the coast whenever his schedule allows.

The Zydeco Minnow started out as a freshwater striper and hybrid pattern. "I gave a few to some clients that fly-fished in saltwater, and got good feedback," he said. "The pattern is a good choice for catching school trout under birds during fall. Because it is a noisy pattern, it is a great fly for blind-casting in deeper water.

"This is a good fly for bad days. Regardless of whether it's extremely cold or muddy water, this fly will catch fish when nothing else works." Woodruff thought the secret lay in what he called "the aggravation factor."

"This fly makes so much noise you can hear it through the hull of your boat. Basically, the fish get tired of all that noise and just hammer it," he said.

When the water is warm, Woodruff retrieves the Zydeco Minnow quickly with 2- to 3-foot strips. In extremely cold or muddy conditions, he uses the same pop-and-pause retrieve, stripping in several inches every 2-3 seconds.

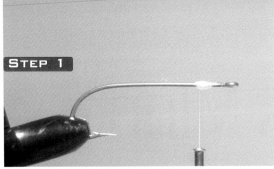

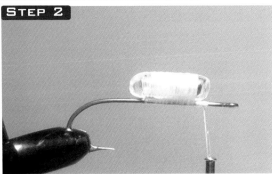

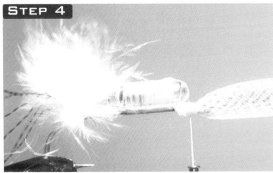

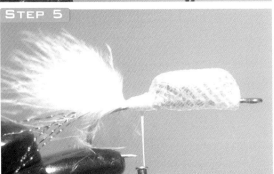

TYING INSTRUCTIONS

STEP 1 Attach thread ⅛ inch from eye.

STEP 2 Spread glue on shank, tie on rattle with firm, even wraps. Coat wraps with glue, allow to dry.

STEP 3 Tie in 10-12 strands Krystal Flash at bend. Add marabou feathers atop flash.

STEP 4 Spiral thread forward to front of rattle. Tie in tubing cut slightly longer than shank, spiral thread to back of rattle.

STEP 5 Gently push braid over rattle with fingers, secure with wraps. Build up tapered tail, tie off.

STEP 6 Figure-8 wrap eyes behind hook eye. Whip finish and cement wraps. Color back side with permanent markers.

VARIATIONS

Captain Woodruff suggested experimenting with your favorite color combinations. He has had quite a bit of success with silver bodies and blue/black backs, pearl bodies with green backs, and gold bodies with black backs and orange bellies.

Steve's Glass Minnow

CAPTAIN STEVE SOULÉ

MATERIALS:

Hook:	Mustad 34007, No. 1, 2, or 4
Thread:	Waxed Danville Flymaster Plus, size A, black
Body:	Mylar tinsel, D-rib, medium
Wing:	Bucktail, white Bucktail, chartreuse

CAPTAIN STEVE SOULÉ, WHO SPENT PART OF HIS YOUTH in Florida fly-fishing for redfish and baby tarpon, started guiding several years ago. "There aren't many fly-fishing guides on the upper Texas coast," Soulé said. "So I decided to give it a try."

Once he moved back to Texas, Soulé started developing patterns for the Galveston Bay complex. Steve's Glass Minnow is a good all-around pattern that is especially deadly when fished under lights.

"Fish can feed much more stealthily at night than they can during the day," Soulé said. "Many times I have stood quietly in the shallows after dark and listened to trout ambushing glass minnows, one of their favorite foods."

Silversides and bay anchovies, collectively known as glass minnows, inhabit Texas bays by the millions. Lights from piers, harbors, and canal communities attract them in huge numbers, creating nocturnal all-you-can-eat buffets.

"I often leave the ramp several hours before dawn so clients can sample some action under the lights," Soulé said. During those early hours, he does not have to compete with the armada of small boats that frequent Galveston Bay, and he slips silently through the dark, allowing his client to cast into the cones of light around docks and canal communities.

"We often catch 50-100 speckled trout before heading off to the flats to sight-cast for redfish," he said. "When fish are aggressively feeding in the lights, you will see and hear them as they smack bait off the surface. When I find them on top, I like to retrieve the fly quickly, using 4- to 8- inch strips. Sometimes you will see the fish in the lights, but they won't come to the surface. Count the fly down 5-8 seconds and retrieve it slowly."

Pick the right night and the action is non-stop. Lightweight rods are well matched to the school-size fish that frequent the illuminated areas. "Since we release many of the fish we catch, I highly recommend mashing down the barb on your hooks so you don't injure them," Soulé suggested.

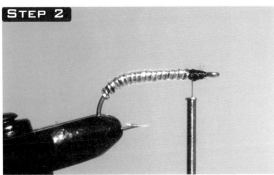

TYING INSTRUCTIONS

STEP 1 Start on shank just forward of point, tie in D-rib. Wrap to ⅛ inch from eye, tie in tinsel.

STEP 2 Wrap tinsel forward to ⅛ inch from eye, slightly overwrapping turns, tie off. Wrap D-rib forward, tie off.

STEP 3 Tie in white bucktail behind eye. Add chartreuse atop white.

STEP 4 Add tinsel strips to sides, whip finish, cement head. Trim tinsel ½ to ¾ of body length

Cypert Minnow

CHARLIE CYPERT

MATERIALS:

Hook:	Mustad 34011, No. 6
Thread:	3/0, chartreuse
Eyes:	Bead chain, small
Body:	Chenille, chartreuse
Overbody:	Mylar cord, size medium

CHARLIE CYPERT BRINGS FIFTY YEARS OF FLY-FISHING experience to the tying bench. If it swims, Cypert has either fished for it or tied a fly that fooled it.

A prolific developer of patterns, Cypert is not content to create a pattern and proclaim good. "I test all of my new patterns in a side-by-side test," he said. "I fish with a partner, and if I catch fish on a new fly, we switch rods. If he or she starts catching more fish than I do, it was a good day for that pattern but it doesn't prove anything. If the new pattern outperforms old standbys on four or five trips using this side-by-side test, I then consider it to be a good pattern." Perhaps this is why Lone Star anglers believe in Cypert's creations.

The Cypert Minnow is one of the patterns that underwent the testing regimen before being released for sale. The little baitfish pattern enjoys widespread popularity, and is sold in most fly shops across the state.

"I developed the Cypert Minnow when they first came out with Mylar tubing back in the 1980s," Cypert said. "This fly is very simple to tie, but it is extremely effective on any fish that eats other fish."

The Cypert Minnow sports a trim profile that makes it easy to cast. The sink rate can be adjusted by varying the size of the eyes. The sparkle of the Mylar tubing makes it especially deadly for speckled trout under lights.

Cypert likes to use what he calls a "crippled baitfish" retrieve. "In nature, fish will strike a crippled baitfish much faster than a healthy one," he explained.

Cypert suggested mixing 4- to 6-inch strips with intermittent pauses to make the pattern look like a cripple struggling through the water.

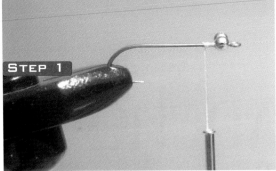

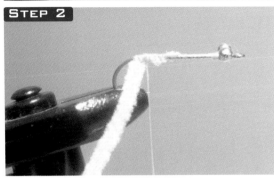

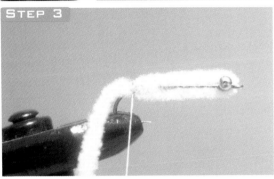

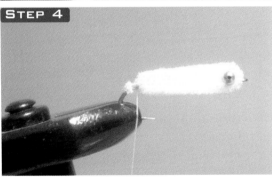

TYING INSTRUCTIONS

STEP 1 Figure-8 wrap eyes near hook eye.

STEP 2 Anchor chenille halfway between eyes and bend. Pull chenille toward bend, wrap around shank, secure with several thread wraps, making sure chenille is on bottom of shank.

STEP 3 Stretch chenille down one side of shank, around the eye on same side, return to bend, anchor at same spot as before.

STEP 4 Repeat Step 3, starting with chenille on top, winding around eyes, anchoring at bend.

STEP 5 Cut enough Mylar to cover back and belly, with extra for tail. Remove inner core, unravel 1 inch at both ends of tubing. Rotate hook point up. Lay tubing belly, anchor at bend. Split tail fibers into 2 bundles, one on either side of hook.

STEP 6 Pull tubing over front of fly back to bend. Place unraveled ends together, pull back to snug tubing, work hook eye through tubing, secure at bend with wraps. Taper thread wraps to match body contour. Trim tail to length.

VARIATIONS

The Cypert Minnow can be tied in many variations. The pattern can be scaled up or down on hook sizes 2-10. For redfish, Cypert prefers a No. 4 or 6 hook. To increase the sink rate, add larger eyes and trim the tail shorter.

Greg's Bay Anchovy

GREG BERLOCHER

MATERIALS:

Hook:	Mustad 34007, No. 4-6
Thread:	Danville Size A, white
Body:	Ultrahair, translucent white
Flash:	Flashabou, pearl
Glue:	5-minute epoxy
Adhesive:	Superglue
Eyes:	4 mm doll eyes

BAY ANCHOVIES ARE SMALL, MINNOW-LIKE BAITFISH THAT inhabit all seven Texas bay systems. They range from 1-4 inches in length. The elongated body is translucent and punctuated by a shiny silver stripe down the lateral line. Although very similar to silversides, bay anchovies are a different species.

Bay anchovies, along with croaker and mullet, are the most abundant species of the bay biomass. At times, speckled trout selectively feed on these fragile baitfish, and often regurgitate them when landed.

Having fished for speckled trout under lights for over 40 years, I sought a good imitation of a bay anchovy without success. Five years of tinkering and on-the-water trial and error led to the final product.

Greg's Bay Anchovy is extremely easy to tie and will catch a variety of fish. In addition to catching Texas spots and specks, friends of mine who live on the East Coast have caught bluefish and striped bass on the pattern. It has also proven successful for fooling dolphin working grass lines in the Gulf.

When speckled trout feed at night under lights, they make a distinctive popping sound. A trout "pop" is a sure sign they are working under the lights.

On a memorable night several years ago near the Arroyo Colorado, I used a Greg's Bay Anchovy to catch and release over 130 speckled trout in about 90 minutes. I had never experienced hand and wrist cramps from catching fish until that night.

Greg's Bay Anchovy is as durable as it is productive. On that memorable night, I landed 63 trout on one fly. Granted, the synthetic wing looked like a fuzzy toothbrush after that many fish, but it was still producing when I clipped it off for sentimental reasons.

The fly can be fished on a floating or sinking line. Cast to the edges of the lights, being careful not to cast shadows on the water. Long, slow strips punctuated with periodic pauses usually bring strikes. Dancing the fly along the surface will also draw speckled trout from the depths.

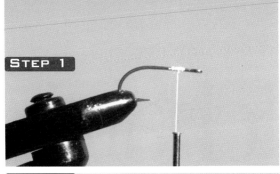

TYING INSTRUCTIONS

STEP 1 Wrap thread base on shank as shown.

STEP 2 Cut 2 hook-length, matchstick-thick bundle Ultrahair. Secure with several loose wraps as shown. Distribute fibers evenly around shank, secure with 10-12 firm wraps.

STEP 3 Add 4 strands of Flashabou to each side of fly, whip finish and trim thread.

STEP 4 Epoxy coat thread wraps lightly, rotate until dry.

STEP 5 Rotate vise 90 degrees. Superglue eyes both sides of head.

STEP 6 Epoxy head, working carefully around eyes. Rotate until dry.

VARIATIONS

Bay anchovies range up to 4 inches long. The pattern can be as tied as small or as large as you want. I always carry a few longer flies and shorten them to the right length on the water.

Although the stripe on the body of a silverside is bright silver, I have had better luck using pearl colored flash rather than silver.

Sparkle Body and stick-on eyes can be used in lieu of epoxy glue and doll eyes.

Haines Pilchard

LARRY HAINES

MATERIALS:

Hook:	Mustad 34007, No. 1/0 or 2/0
Thread:	Uni 6/0, white
Head:	Large gold cone
Wing:	Supreme Hair, white
	Supreme Hair, chartreuse
	Fly Fur, chartreuse
Flash:	Flashabou or Sparkleflash, silver
Belly:	Polarbear Neer Hair
Gills:	Flashabou or Sparkleflash, gold
Eyes:	Doll eyes or 1/4-inch silver prismatic eyes
Glue:	Flexament Devcon 5-minute epoxy

A NATIVE OF SOUTH TEXAS AND CO-OWNER OF THE SHOP in Port Isabel, Larry Haines has been fly-fishing in the salt close to twenty years. He and his fishing partner get together two or three times per week in pursuit of different prey. One of their favorites is snook.

South Texas boasts the only viable fishery in the state for this semi-tropical fish. Venues such as the Brownsville Ship Channel and the Port Isabel jetties are well documented as snook hangouts.

Haines stressed the importance of strong tidal movement when targeting snook. "The fish feed when the tide is the strongest," he said.

South Texas snook have a habit of holding in very deep water, making it difficult for fly-fishermen to get a pattern deep enough to connect. Haines set out to solve this by creating a baitfish pattern with a quick sink rate.

"The cone head allows the Haines Pilchard to dive quickly when you stop stripping," he said. "Plus, it has a nice jigging action when you strip it. The fish really slam this fly. There will be no doubt in your mind when you have a strike."

Haines fishes the jetties quite a bit with the Haines Pilchard, and has noted that the pattern's quick sink rate makes it hang in the rocks if you do not pay attention. He suggested a quick retrieve using 1- to 2-foot strips. A Haines Pilchard fished on clear intermediate line equipped with a 5-foot leader can easily reach depths of 15 feet.

In addition to jetty fishing, Haines loves to drive the beaches of South Padre Island and seek action in deep guts between the waterline and the first bar. While standing on the sand, he has caught kingfish, tarpon, bull reds, and jackfish on the Haines Pilchard. Keep several of these flies in your box when you need a baitfish pattern that can get down deep.

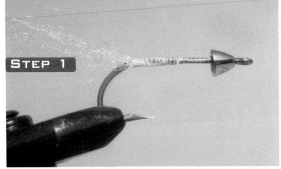

TYING INSTRUCTIONS

STEP 1 Bend down barb, slip on cone as shown. With hook point down, tie a 2-inch, matchstick-thick bundle white Supreme Hair atop shank. ("Taperize" ends after each step to create a tapered look. Avoid "toothbrush" appearance at ends.) Flexament in place.

STEP 2 Rotate vise, tie second 2-inch white hair bundle forward of first. Secure to shank, make wraps between bundle and hook so hair angles out. Flexament wraps.

STEP 3 Repeat Step 2 until cone is reached, rotating vise as needed. Add Flashabou to both sides; length to end of hair.

STEP 4 With hook point up, tie 1½-inch Neer Hair to form belly, taperize.

STEP 5 With hook point down, add gold flash to back, trim to length of white Supreme Hair. Tie 3½-inch bundle chartreuse Supreme Hair atop gold flash. Rotate fly on side, add ¾-inch bundle gold flash. Repeat on other side. Tie ¾-inch bundle chartreuse Fly Fur atop chartreuse Supreme Hair. Whip finish, taperize.

STEP 6 Epoxy eyes on head as shown, rotate until dry.

Mirro-Mullet

REGGIE SHEFFIELD

MATERIALS:

Hook:	Mustad 34007 or TMC 811s, No. 1, 2 or 4
Thread:	Danville Flymaster Plus, white
Eyes:	Umpqua or Wapsi alloy eyes
Flash:	Krystal Flash, chartreuse Krystal Flash, black
Body:	Ram's wool, white Ram's wool, rust

"I HAD SEEN WOOLHEAD PATTERNS BEFORE," SAID REGGIE Sheffield of Houston. "But they were all just too big to use for sight-casting in shallow water. Plus, when those large flies got wet, they weren't much fun to cast."

After a little tinkering at the vise, Sheffield found that a smaller woolhead pattern tied on a No. 4 hook was just right for the Texas coast, and the Mirro-Mullet was born.

The Mirro-Mullet derives its name from the famed L & S Lures MirrOLure. Sheffield's days of slinging hard-bodied plugs with conventional tackle convinced him that a baitfish pattern that would suspend in the strike zone would be very successful.

Sheffield favors the Mirro-Mullet when fishing over grass beds. The little woolhead sinks very slowly and does not go straight to the bottom like weighted flies. Plus, the large bulky profile pushes a lot of water when stripped.

"I wanted something that had a lot of presence in the water," Sheffield said. "Fish sometimes have a hard time seeing flies with narrow profiles in thick grass.

"The Mirro-Mullet should be fished in knee deep water or less, varying the retrieve between fast and slow to imitate a crippled baitfish. You want the fly to look like a food item to the fish."

Before casting the Mirro-Mullet to a prospective fish, Sheffield suggested wetting the fly thoroughly as the wool takes a while to absorb water. "The Mirro-Mullet has much better action once it's wet," he said.

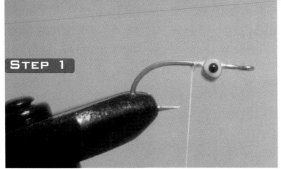

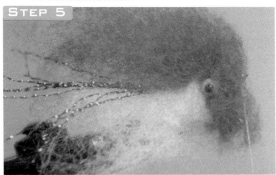

TYING INSTRUCTIONS

STEP 1 With hook point up, tie 2 thread bumps on shank as shown. Figure-8 wrap eyes in place between bumps. Rotate vise, hook point down.

STEP 2 Fold 3 strands chartreuse Krystal Flash around thread, tie behind eyes. Repeat on other side. Fold 4 strands black Krystal Flash around thread, tie behind eyes. Repeat on other side. Nip flash ends different lengths to taper-ize.

STEP 3 Rotate vise, hook point up. Hold small tuft white ram's wool parallel to shank, tie behind eyes with 2 tight wraps. Head cement thread wraps. Pull back wool ends, forming belly and tail.

STEP 4 Rotate vise, hook point down. Hold bundle colored wool parallel to shank, tie behind eyes with 2 tight wraps. Pull back wool ends, forming tail. Anchor wool with 2 wraps. Head cement thread wraps. Wrap thread forward to eye.

STEP 5 Hold another bundle colored wool between finger and thumb and "center punch" over eye, distributing evenly around shank. Make 2 thread wraps around wool between eyes and hook eye, pull down tight. Maintaining tension on thread, pull thread forward through wool to eye, tie off. Cement head. Pull wool extending past hook eye toward tail, smooth to shape.

STEP 6 Remove fly from vise, hold by tail wool. Trim belly flat with curved scissors. Trim head to resemble small mullet. Eyes should be just visible through the wool. Taper body. Thin tail so Krystal Flash shines through.

VARIATIONS

The Mirro-Mullet can be tied with solid white ram's wool, sometimes called sculpin wool, and colored with a marker in lieu of using separate colors. Sheffield suggested this approach when first learning the pattern.

Phillips Header

CAPTAIN CHRIS PHILLIPS

MATERIALS:

Hook:	Tiemco 8011s, No. 1/0
Thread:	Flay wax nylon, white
Tail:	6 saddle hackles, yellow
	8 strands of peacock herl
	Flashabou, 10 strands, red
	Bucktail
Body:	E-Z Body, size large, pearl
Eyes:	Red hologram, 5/16 inch
Glue:	5-minute epoxy
Gills/body	Permanent markers

YOU MAY NOT KNOW CAPTAIN CHRIS PHILLIPS, BUT chances are you have seen him on the cover of a well-known coastal fishing map that covers the middle Texas coast. The map jacket features Captain Phillips holding a nice redfish and the fly rod it was caught on.

Look closely at that picture and you will notice that the reel is a Pflueger Medalist--not your typical saltwater reel. "Other than Billy Pate tarpon reels, there weren't any saltwater fly reels back then," Phillips said.

Twenty-five years have passed since that photo was taken, and there is now an abundance of fly-fishing equipment up to the challenge of the salt. One thing hasn't changed though: as one friend put it, Phillips is still "Lean as a stick of beef jerky."

A big trout specialist who plies the waters of the Galveston Bay system, Phillips is the first to remind everyone that big trout prefer big mullet. For many years, Phillips threw large Deceivers with good results, but the long hackles used in the tail would sometimes foul around the hook.

"In over 20 years of fly-fishing, I never had a fish eat a fouled fly," Phillips said. He also noted the tapered head of a Deceiver does not resemble the broad, bulbous head of a mullet.

The introduction of braided tubing several years ago led to the creation of this imaginative pattern. "There isn't a fly around that has the action of a Deceiver," Phillips said. "Adding tubing to the body solved the fouling problem while preserving the action of the fly. Plus, the tubing creates a more realistic head."

The Phillips Header is a great choice when blind-casting for trophy trout in the winter and spring. It is best fished in knee- to waist-deep water. In cold water, Phillips suggested slow, short strips with frequent pauses. In warmer water, go with longer 9- to 12-inch strips.

Phillips has also had tremendous success using the Phillips Header offshore in the Gulf of Mexico. The pat-

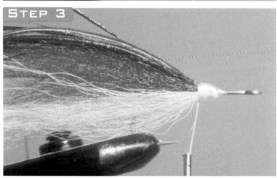

tern has fooled cobia (ling), shark, kingfish, and dorado (dolphin).

TYING INSTRUCTIONS

STEP 1 Tie saddle hackles mid-point of shank. Add 10 strands red Flashabou.

STEP 2 Rotate vise, hook point up. (Not shown.) Add bundle, ½ pencil thickness, yellow bucktail collar. Rotate vise, hook point down. Add equivalent amount red bucktail to complete collar.

STEP 3 Top red bucktail with peacock herl.

STEP 4 Measure tubing length against hook. Cut to length, careful to avoid unraveling. (A cauterizing pen or soldering iron will cut tubing and seal ends in one step.) Turn tubing partially inside-out, place over eye of hook, secure neatly to shank.

STEP 5 Roll tubing onto fly, adjust feathers and bucktail as needed.

STEP 6 Epoxy eyes to tubing. Add counter shading and gills with permanent markers.

VARIATIONS

The Phillips Header is easy to modify and can be tied in a number of color combinations. Some of the most popular include red/yellow, red/white, blue/white, and chartreuse/white. If fishing in turbid conditions, a small rattle can be tucked into the tubing body.

Scissor Tail Clouser

CHARLIE CYPERT

MATERIALS:

Hook:	Mustad 34007 or 34011, No. 6
Thread:	3/0, chartreuse
Weedguard	10- to 20-pound Hard Mason
Eyes:	Bead chain
Tail:	Two or four salt-water saddle hackles
Body:	Flashabou, pearl
Belly:	Bucktail, white
Back:	Bucktail, chartreuse
Cement:	Head cement, clear

CHARLIE CYPERT'S FLIES HAVE CAUGHT FISH ALL OVER the world, and his creations have been featured in four national fly-fishing magazines. A half-century of fly-fishing experience under his belt backs up his opinions.

One of Cypert's axioms is that "less is more" when fishing in clear water. He has demonstrated repeatedly that sparsely tied patterns produce far more than an identical fly that is dressed more fully.

The Scissor Tail Clouser is one of Cypert's best know patterns. A modification to the renowned Clouser Minnow, Cypert substituted hackles in lieu of bucktail to give the pattern more movement in the water.

Cypert learned a valuable lesson one night while crappie fishing with conventional tackle under lights. "You could see down into the water quite a ways, and there were thousands of shad milling about," he recalled. "Every now and then, a crippled shad would swim through the lights and instantly be attacked by a crappie."

Observing this, Cypert began mimicking the crippled baitfish with his jig. Ninety-six crappie later, he was convinced that a crippled baitfish retrieve would trigger far more strikes than a normal retrieve.

"Over the years, I caught large numbers of fish on Clouser Minnows, but I never caught that many big fish," Cypert told me. "So I started wondering why."

It turned out to be a fairly simple answer. The bucktail used in Clouser Minnows is fairly stiff and does not have much action. By substituting hackles for the bucktail, Cypert was better able to imitate a wounded or dying baitfish. Large fish will shadow a school of smaller fish and pick off cripples that the others miss.

"The Scissor Tail Clouser will appeal to those larger fish," he said. "Too many anglers are mechanical when stripping a pattern. The idea is to make the fly appear to be injured or disoriented."

Cypert suggested a pop-and-pause, followed by a pop-pop and another pause, of 1-2 seconds to allow the fly to fall, which triggers many strikes.

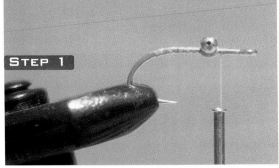

TYING INSTRUCTIONS

STEP 1 Figure-8 wrap eyes as shown. Add optional weedguard at bend.

STEP 2 Select 4 hackles 1½ - 2 times hook length, turn to splay outward, anchor behind eyes. Wrap thread to bend.

STEP 3 Wind thread back to eyes, anchor 4-6 strands pearl Flashabou. Wind Flashabou around shank to bend then back to eyes in overlapping spirals. Tie off and trim. Head cement body with even coat.

STEP 4 Tie white bucktail bundle at hook eye, secure with wraps both sides of eyes.

STEP 5 Rotate vise, hook point up. Tie 6-8 strands pearl Flashabou ahead of eyes, extending full body length on both sides.

STEP 6 Rotate vise, hook point down. Tie chartreuse bucktail ahead of eyes. Tie optional weedguard near hook eye. Build up tapered head with thread, whip finish, tie off. Cement head.

VARIATIONS

The Scissor Tail Clouser can be tied in any color combination you like. Some of Cypert's favorites for saltwater include red/white, chartreuse/white, gray/white, and pink/white.

The pattern can be tied on any hook between No. 6 and 2/0. Adjust the size of the eyes to vary sink rate. Cypert favors a weedguard because it keeps the hackles from fouling around the hook.

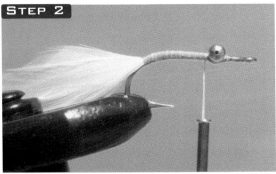

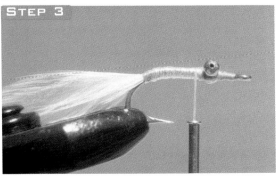

CHAPTER 3
Crab Patterns

Baby Stingray Crab

JERRY LORING

MATERIALS:

Hook:	Mustad 34007, No. 4
Thread:	Number 3 thread, any color
Eyes:	lead dumbbell, 4/32-ounce
Claws:	Flashabou, red & blue
	Fish Hair, olive or marabou
Body:	Furry Foam, olive
Glue:	Waterproof glue

JERRY LORING IS THE UNOFFICIAL AMBASSADOR OF HOUSTON- based Texas Fly Fishers, the largest fly-fishing club in the state. Known affectionately as "Buggywhip" to his fellow club members, he routinely absorbs their velvet barbs during meetings and outings. Loring helps organize many of the club's saltwater outings, including the Redfish Rodeo, which is the largest catch-and-release saltwater fly-fishing tournament in the state.

Over the years, Loring noticed that many redfish would turn away from swimming patterns. The fish were either not interested in that type of fly, or were spooked by it. Through experimentation, Loring discovered that bottom flies tend to spook redfish less than any other pattern. He also noted that many of the reds he cleaned were full of 1-inch crabs.

At the time, the only well-known crab patterns were the Merkin Crab and the McCrab. Both patterns were too much of an investment in time for the high-energy Loring, and he set out to find a simple crab pattern that was quick and easy to tie. The pattern got its name when author Phil Shook noted that Loring's new pattern looked like a baby stingray.

Early versions of the pattern featured lead eyes tied near the eye of the hook. After a little "rod time," Loring found that tying the eyes mid-ship would allowed the fly to settle on top of sea grass rather than fall down into it--a definite advantage when trying to get fish to notice your offering. When the pattern does sink into the growth, the broad shape of the carapace tends to push most of the grass away from the fly, making it fairly weedless.

Loring favors the Baby Stingray Crab on flats that have a mixture of sand and grass. He suggested casting the fly 3-4 feet in front of singles or doubles and retrieving at a dead-slow crawl.

"Go as slow as your nerves allow when you see a red," he said. "If the fish turns away, pick up the fly immediately and cast again."

Loring noted that redfish will often pick up a Baby Stingray Crab and casually swim off. "You may never feel

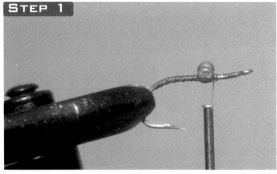

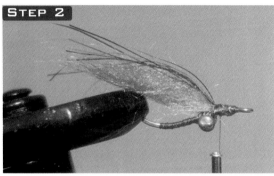

a strike, only the line going tight," he said.

If you find tailing fish, Loring suggested casting the Baby Stingray Crab right into the school and begin the dead-slow retrieve. Strikes will often be more aggressive in this situation.

TYING INSTRUCTIONS

STEP 1 Bend hook eye away from point 15 degrees. Base-wrap shank, eye to bend. Figure-8 wrap eyes between hook eye and point as shown.

STEP 2 Rotate vise, hook point up. Tie hook-length Fish Hair (or marabou) tuft above eyes. Tie 8 strands red and blue Flashabou atop Fish Hair, tie off.

STEP 3 Split Fish Hair and Flashabou into two sections with bodkin. Figure-8 wrap to 45-degree angles. Whip finish, do not form tapered head. (Vise in photo rotated 90 degree only to show detail.)

STEP 4 Cut Furry Foam crab-shaped, less than 1 inch tip-to-tip width. Glue atop eyes under hook point.

VARIATIONS

The Baby Stingray Crab can be tied in a number of different color combinations to match different crab species. Furry Foam in tan, green, and brown are good options for the carapace. Try different combinations of Flashabou, including red/gold and blue/green. Loring sometimes uses rubber legs and mallard flank feathers in lieu of Fish Hair.

Blue Crab

ROY WILLIAMS

MATERIALS:

Hook:	Mustad 34007, No. 4
Thread:	Danville flat waxed nylon, black
Tail:	Arctic fox, olive Krystal Flash, blue & pearl
Eyes:	U-shaped mono with burned tips Extra small lead dumbbell eyes
Body:	Hackles, blue & olive
Claw tips:	Arctic fox, orange

ROY WILLIAMS WAS A PROFESSOR OF ENGINEERING AT THE University of Houston before he retired and moved to Rockport. Since retirement, he has been quite busy tying and designing new patterns for the locals guides.

Not surprising, Williams brings an engineering mind-set to the design process. Sitting down with a guide, he listens to their ideas then sketches out a prototype with colored pencils. Once the general design and color are agreed on, it is off to the tying bench.

Williams even developed a special scale for weighing flies. "I assumed that flies that weigh the same will have the same approximate sink rate," he explained. "Since we fish a lot over shallow grass beds, the sink rate of a fly will either make or break it. I weighed a lot of successful patterns and try to replicate those weights.

"The Rockport area has a large crab hatch during the spring, but all the crab patterns I found were just too heavy to cast. Blue crabs are the predominant species in our bays, so I studied them extensively before designing the pattern. While at rest or in a defensive posture, the crab's blue claws, tipped with reddish orange, were very obvious.

"After I developed the pattern, I experimented with different weights for different conditions. I use lead eyes when fishing on sand or soft mud, but bead chain eyes are a better choice for fishing over grass because it minimizes the sink rate."

Williams suggested bumping the fly along the bottom using short 4- to 6-inch strips. "It really depends on the fish," he said. "I change my retrieve if the fish don't like what I am doing."

Williams suggested using a loop knot when fishing the Blue Crab.

He made an interesting side note involving the color blue. He felt brightly colored flies will spook fish in extremely shallow water--except blue ones. "For some reason, blue doesn't seem to bother redfish at all," he noted.

The professor also held forth on weedguards, saying flatly, "I don't like them, and neither do most of the

STEP 1

STEP 2

STEP 3

STEP 4

STEP 5

STEP 6

guides. They can interfere with a solid hook set." Williams estimated that you get 50 percent less hookups when a weedguard is used.

"There are a lot of opinions out there about fly-fishing, but only one judge, and that is Mr. Redfish. I will let him decide," Williams declared.

TYING INSTRUCTIONS

STEP 1 Tie shank-length thread base. Tie olive fox hair bundle perpendicular to shank. Tie flash atop fox hair, form both into split tail. Trim to ½ inch.

STEP 2 Tie lead eyes near hook eye. Rotate vise, hook point up. Figure-8 wrap U-shaped eyes center shank.

STEP 3 Tie and palmer blue hackle under hook point. Tie olive hackle ahead of blue hackle on eyes side.

STEP 4 Add small bundle orange fox, laying wraps centered between U-shaped eyes. Wind thread forward.

STEP 5 Palmer hackle between and around mono eyes, tie off.

STEP 6 Tie and palmer blue hackle between mono and lead eyes. Whip finish, head cement wraps.

Crystal Crab

BILL GAMMEL

MATERIALS:

Hook:	Mustad 34011, No. 6
Thread:	Size 3/0, olive
Weedguard (Optional)	30-pound Hard Mason mono
Claws:	Marabou, olive
Lead wire:	.125 diameter
Inner legs/Eyes:	Live Rubber, 2 strips
Legs:	Live Rubber, 1 strip
Body:	Crystal Chenille

CASTING NEXT TO BILL GAMMEL IS LIKE TEEING OFF NEXT TO Tiger Woods. Fly-fishing since he was seven years old and teaching fly-fishermen how to cast since he was 15, Gammel now serves on the Federation of Fly Fishers (FFF) Board of Governors for Casting Certification. That places him in the select company of roughly 30 people worldwide with similar casting skills.

Because of Gammel's surgeon-like precision with a fly rod, he is a sought-after instructor and speaker at public events. Fly rod manufacturers seek out his advice as well.

With that in mind, it does not stretch the imagination why Gammel developed the Crystal Crab. "Most crab patterns are very difficult to cast," he explained. "My goal was to develop a pattern that you could cast accurately, make a quiet presentation, wasn't intricate to tie, and still gave a reasonably good impression of a crab.

"Whether I am casting to a cruising redfish or to a pothole in the grass, I am always aiming at specific targets. Many times, redfish will be lying in the grass near a sand spot, but aren't in an aggressive mood. Baitfish patterns have to stripped fairly quickly to avoid fouling in the sea grass. Before the fish can react, the fly is gone. The only alternative is to let the fly sink to the bottom--but a Clouser Minnow doesn't look very life-like sitting on the bottom."

Although it is very light, the Crystal Crab presents a good crab-like silhouette. One of Gammel's favorite techniques for fishing it is to cast to the far edge of a pothole and let it sink. He then crawls the patterns very slowly across the sand bottom, often taking six or more seconds to retrieve 12 inches of line, giving the fish ample time to react to the fly.

Gammel has had the best luck using the Crystal Crab during the summer over sand and mud bottoms. When the water is very clear and fish are tailing, he fishes it over grass.

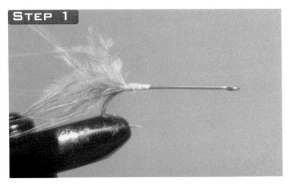

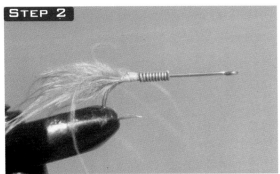

TYING INSTRUCTIONS

STEP 1 Tie threadbase near bend as shown. Pluck marabou barbules from stem, tie on thread base.

STEP 2 Wrap 4-6 turns lead wire from thread base toward eye.

STEP 3 (Vise in photo rotated only to show detail.) Strip 2-3 rubber ribs for inside legs and eyes, single rib for outside legs. Tie overhand knot in wide sections to make eyes, ensuring eyes "point" outward. Trim rubber. Figure-8 wrap inside leg, bottom of shank. Space other legs evenly and secure. Tie outside legs at both shank ends.

STEP 4 (Vise in photo rotated only to show detail.) Figure-8 wrap marabou claw to stand perpendicular to shank.

STEP 5 (Vise in photo rotated only to show detail.) Tie Crystal Chenille as shown, wind thread forward, then wind short section of chenille forward to eye. Tie off, whip finish.

VARIATIONS

The Crystal Crab can also be tied with tan or brown Crystal Chenille.

Mud Crab

CAPTAIN BILL HAGEN

MATERIALS:

Hook:	Mustad 34007, No. 6
Thread:	Flymaster Plus, tan
Bead:	Brass bead, small
Tail:	Craft fur
Eyes:	Burned mono eyes, 32 pound Hard Mason
Body:	Aunt Lydia's Rug Yarn, crème
	Aunt Lydia's Rug Yarn, brown
Cement:	Flexament
	Devcon 5-minute epoxy
Weed guard:	10 pound Hard Mason
Paint:	Oil based model paint, black

CAPTAIN BILL HAGEN IS A MASTER AT MATCHING THE hatch. The crab hatch, that is.

According to Texas Parks & Wildlife Department biologists, 92 different species of crabs inhabit Texas bay and Gulf waters. The blue crab is by far the most recognized arthropod in Texas bays. Other 8-legged bay dwellers include the sand, fiddler, and mud crabs.

An inspection of stomach contents from one of Hagen's catches revealed the fish had been feeding exclusively on tiny mud crabs. He set out to craft a credible facsimile.

"Most crab flies cast like a brick," Hagen said. "I wanted to develop something that you could actually cast rather than lob at the fish."

Aunt Lydia's Rug Yarn is one of Hagen's favorite tying materials because it is easy to work with and extremely durable. After a little tweaking, the Mud Crab took up permanent resident in his fly box.

"When small crabs want to move a great distance, they get just below the surface and ride the current," he explained. "When threatened, the little crabs dive quickly to the bottom to hide."

Rather than use traditional lead dumbbell eyes for weight, Captain Hagen substituted a small brass bead near the hook eye. The body is very thin and streamlined, so as not to hinder the sink rate. The design allows the pattern to dive quickly while remaining very light.

Fishing a crab pattern is different than a baitfish or shrimp pattern. Hagen suggested casting the Mud Crab ahead of tailing or cruising fish, and slowly stripping it across the bottom until the fish sees it. Then stop all movement and let it sit. Typically, a redfish will rush the fly and eat it.

Although Hagen fishes the Mud Crab year-around it, is one of his confidence patterns during the late spring

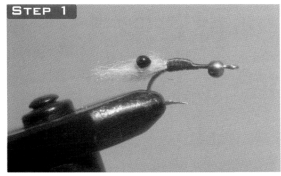

when there are large numbers of crab hatches. "If you are working hard trying to get the fish to eat and getting refusals on shrimp and baitfish patterns, it is time to try a crab pattern," he advised.

TYING INSTRUCTIONS

STEP 1 Place brass bead on shank. Tie small tuft craft fur as shown. Burn mono tips to round shape, coat with paint-tinted epoxy, let dry, tie in.

STEP 2 (Vise in photo rotated 90 degrees only to show detail.) Figure-8 wrap to shank pieces of Aunt Lydia's Rug Yarn, alternating brown and crème colors.

STEP 3 (Vise in photo rotated 90 degrees only to show detail.) Fill shank with yarn.

STEP 4 (Vise in photo rotated 90 degrees only to show detail.) Thin and trim yarn to shape, coat with Flexament, add weedguard.

Parachute Crab

LARRY SUNDERLAND

MATERIALS:

Hook:	Tiemco or Gamakatsu, No. 2-8
Thread:	3/0, red
Eyes:	Bead chain, plastic
Claws:	2 grizzly hackles, neck
Body:	Large grizzly saddle hackle Rams wool, gray and olive
Glue:	Head cement

LARRY SUNDERLAND, OWNER OF THE AUSTIN ANGLER, DOES not mince words when describing why he likes to catch redfish on a fly rod. "The more challenging it is to catch a fish, the more entertaining it is," he said.

Sunderland has been fly-fishing the Texas coast for 12 years and has developed several innovative saltwater patterns.

Sunderland's Parachute Crab is one of his patterns developed for a specific situation. "During the fall, there are some incredible crab hatches," he said. "I would see wads of thumbnail-sized crabs being pulled along the surface by a strong tide, but there was only an inch of water covering the sea grass. I spent too much time pulling grass off traditional crab patterns."

The pattern gets its name from a hackle which is wound around the eyes and extends downward like a parachute. The fly is easy to tie; a skilled hand taking no more than 3-4 minutes to complete.

The Parachute Crab is so light you can fish it in a heavy dew. In many ways, fishing the little crab pattern is like dry-fly fishing. "The shallower the better," Sunderland said. "Nothing is as exciting as watching a big red come up and sip the fly off the film."

"This pattern is not a good choice for early morning fishing. "It really works better once the sun has risen in the sky a bit and the fish can see it. If they see it, they usually eat it."

Sunderland favors the Parachute Crab when targeting redfish or black drum. He suggested casting it right on the nose of a feeding fish. He cautioned against moving the pattern too much once you make your presentation. "People have a tendency to move it too fast or too far," he noted. "Small crabs don't naturally move 12 inches in the blink of an eye."

Sunderland selects patterns tied with plastic eyes for shallow water duty, but opts for either bead chain or

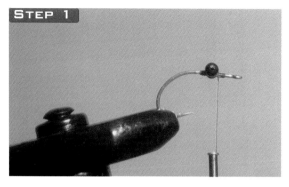

lead eyes when he wants to go deep. "I typically use bead chain eyes when fishing in calf- to knee-deep water," he said. "The sinking version is a great choice for fishing over mud bottoms. Once you cast, make 3-4 very slow strips then pause before repeating."

TYING INSTRUCTIONS

STEP 1 Figure-8 wrap eyes as shown. Cement wraps.

STEP 2 Tie two 3-hook-length grizzly hackles by butts behind eyes. Tie long, webby hackle by tip behind eyes.

STEP 3 Tie 2 claw hackles at 90 degrees. Wind hackle around eyes and shank to hook eye, forming parachute. (Do not figure-8 wrap hackle; wind above one eye then under shank. Correctly wound hackle will be on side opposite hook point.)

STEP 4 Rotate vise, hook point up. Mix 2 small bunches olive and gray ram's wool. Hold wool atop eyes, wrap in middle, tighten thread (process similar to stacking deer hair). Wind thread forward, avoiding wool and hackles. Tie off at eye, whip finish.

STEP 5 Lift wool straight up, clip with scissors to creates dome-shaped body. Tease body to shape as needed Finished body is ¾ inch diameter.

VARIATIONS

The Parachute Crab can be tied with plastic, bead chain or lead eyes. Cream or brown ram's wool can be used in lieu of olive.

Profile Crab

CAPTAIN SKIPPER RAY

MATERIALS:

Hook:	Mustad 34011, No. 4
Thread:	White
Eyes:	Plastic bead chain or burned mono
Body:	Chenille, white
Pinchers:	Grizzly hackles, red Grizzly hackles, white
Wing:	Bucktail, white Bucktail, green

CAPTAIN SKIPPER RAY OF PORT ISABEL WON THE TEXAS International Fishing Tournament (TIFT) in 1999, which speaks well of his fishing skills. Not only did he walk away with the fly-fishing crown that year, he was the Grand Champion of the whole tournament, putting him in select company. In the 60-plus year history of the south Texas tournament, a fly-fisherman had never won it. Pretty impressive, when you consider Ray was competing with over 1,600 bait and lure fishermen that year.

A keen observer of the marine environment, Ray explained that redfish cruising shallow shorelines are often keying in on crabs. "Especially, if there isn't any other bait in the area," he said.

Ray ties all of the patterns his clients use. "My first goal was to create a pattern you could cast easily with a 6- or 7-weight rod," he said. "And, I wanted a crab fly that would be appealing from either side." Hence the name, Profile Crab, because it looks the same viewed from the right or left.

Ray favors the fly in the spring and early summer, when crab hatches are plentiful. "A fleeing crab swims sideways to escape a predator," he explained. "They swim in a straight line and don't bob up and down while swimming. When stripping the Profile Crab, make long, slow strips a foot to a foot-and-a-half long, barely pausing between strips. It is important to keep the fly at the same depth so it will appear natural."

Ray suggested a clinch knot in lieu of a loop knot to keep the fly from bouncing during the retrieve.

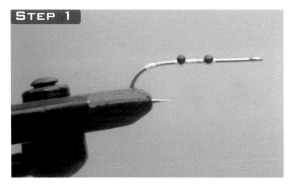

TYING INSTRUCTIONS

STEP 1 Center eyes between hook eye and bend, ⅜ inch apart, secure in place.

STEP 2 Rotate vise, hook point up. Tie white chenille at bend. Tie 1 red, 1 white ¾-inch hackle tips near eye, angling backward. Repeat near bend with remaining hackles. Wind thread to hook eye. Grasp and break red hackle stem with tweezers, forming V to simulate claw.

STEP 3 Wrap chenille forward to eye, avoiding hackles, tie off.

STEP 4 Add white bucktail wing, top with green bucktail. Whip finish, cement head.

VARIATIONS

Orange hackles can be substituted for red.

CHAPTER 4
Bendbacks

Hot Butt Bendback

CAPTAIN CHUCK SCATES

MATERIALS:

Hook:	Mustad 34007, No. 1 or 2
Thread:	White
Body:	Chenille, white & hot pink
Wing:	Hackle feathers, white
Tail:	Bucktail, white
Flash:	Crystal Flash
Topping:	Peacock herl

CAPTAIN CHUCK SCATES OF ROCKPORT HOLDS THE CURRENT IGFA record for seatrout (speckled trout) on 2-pound tippet. On 8 July 1989, he landed a mammoth 8-pound, 11-ounce speck on a fly rod and secured a hallowed place in Texas fly-fishing lore.

Scates has guided fly-fisherman for so long, many folks do not realize he was a successful guide with conventional tackle in a previous life. "Back then, the hot lure was a soft plastic shrimp tail dipped in paint," he said. "Those lures were, and still are, effective, because they imitate shrimp, which have colored tail sections. Coastal fishermen often refer to this style shrimp tail generically as 'firetail'.

"I had never seen a fly pattern with this type of coloration, so I decided to experiment. That was the genesis of the Hot Butt Bendback."

Using the general design characteristics of the bendback pattern popularized by fly-fishing legend Chico Fernandez, Scates experimented with a number of color combinations. A white body with a hot pink butt section turned out to be a consistent producer.

"I fish bendbacks all year long," Scates said. "They are one of the most versatile and productive patterns you can fish on the Texas coast."

Indeed, bendbacks are a popular choice with coastal fishermen. Their light weight often makes them a better choice than bulky, wind-resistance patterns. The hook rides point-up, which keeps them from snagging on obstructions. Since the hair wing covers the hook point, bendbacks are virtually weedless, making them a great choice for thick grass beds.

Scates fishes the Hot Butt Bendback a number of ways. "Depending on what the fish respond to, I may bump it along the bottom, drag it through the grass, or ride it along the surface," he said. "If a redfish is rooting around on the bottom, I fish it deeper so the fish can see it."

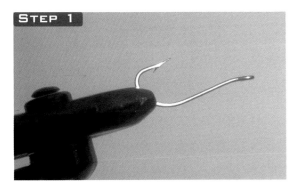

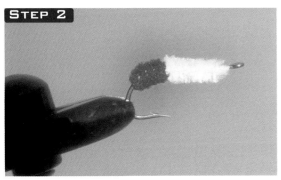

TYING INSTRUCTIONS

STEP 1 Bend hook away from barb near eye.

STEP 2 Tie hot pink chenille near bend, make 3-4 forward wraps, tie off. Tie white chenille as shown, wrap to eye, tie off.

STEP 3 Rotate vise. Match 4 equal-size hackle feathers, tie in at eye, arrange on both sides of hook point.

STEP 4 Tie in several strands Crystal Flash.

STEP 5 Add bucktail collar around hackles.

STEP 6 Top wings with peacock herl strands.

VARIATIONS

The Hot Butt Bendback can be tied in a variety of contrasting colors, including red, chartreuse, black, and pink.

Mr. Pinky

CAPTAIN ERIC GLASS

MATERIALS:

Hook:	Tiemco 811s, No. 6
Thread:	Danville Plus, black
Body:	Medium chenille, pink
Wing:	Bucktail, dark red
Flash:	Flashabou, red
Glue:	Superglue

CAPTAIN ERIC GLASS IS ONE OF THE MOST RECOGNIZED names on the Texas fly-fishing scene. A former biology teacher who gave up an indoor classroom for an outdoor one, he is well respected when it comes to fishing the salt.

Having been a fixture in South Texas for many years, you may be surprised to find that he grew up in Pasadena, Texas, and learned to fly-fish for bass and crappie in golf course water hazards.

He made the switch to saltwater while in high school. "Back in 1983, there weren't a lot of saltwater patterns available," he said. "So I started tying my own. When I was a senior in high school, I read an article by Chico Fernandez about fishing bendback flies over grass flats. After that, I started experimenting with different color bendbacks in the Rockport area. Mr. Pinky was the result of a lot of trial and error."

Glass felt that trout and reds like Mr. Pinky because it creates a general silhouette of a shrimp as it darts through the water.

Although Glass wade-fishes with most of his clients, he described an interesting drill when checking out a shallow flat. "We have so many fishy areas in Lower Laguna Madre that it would take forever to wade in and check them all out," he said. "To save time, I like to pole the boat into a promising area and scope it out. If we find fish, we stop. If there aren't any fish around, I pole the boat out into deeper water before cranking up my engine. Because I don't spook the fish with my engine, I can go back to the same spots time after time and the fish will still be there.

"While poling or drifting in search of fish, we usually get a few shots, so it is best to be ready. "A drifting boat is much easier for the fish to see, and you don't get much time before the fish spook. I tell clients to cast one foot in front of a cruising fish and immediately start stripping the fly. You want to give the fish the impression that the fly is going to vanish in an instant, creating an impulse to eat it right now. If they ignore it or turn away, you should cast again."

TYING INSTRUCTIONS

STEP 1 Bend hook away from point at eye. Tie chenille to shank even with barb, carry thread wraps forward as shown. Wrap chenille forward, tie off leaving space for wing near eye.

STEP 2 Select dark red, almost black 2-hook-length fibers from middle of bucktail, tie wing.

STEP 3 Add 4 strands Flashabou to each side. Build small, neat head, whip finish. Superglue head.

CHAPTER 5
Attractor Patterns

Bead Eye Roadkill

MARK PETRIE

MATERIALS:

Hook:	Mustad 34007, No. 4 or 6
Thread:	6/0, black
Tail:	Grizzly saddle hackles, yellow
Flash:	Flashabou & Krystal Flash, gold
Body:	Grizzly saddle hackles, yellow
Eyes:	Medium bead chain, black

A COMMERCIAL AND CUSTOM TIER, MARK PETRIE NOT only supplies patterns for fly shops across Texas, but also ties flies for exhibitions. Speak with him for a while about fly-tying, and you immediately appreciate the sense of history he brings to the vise.

"Feathers available commercially today are completely different than they were just 50 years ago," he said. "Since most of the chickens have been genetically bred to produce trout flies, hackles are much different now. I have a collection of old necks dating to the 1950s, and they have webs that are extremely wide and go all the way to the tip. I use those feathers only in exhibition flies."

Petrie reached back into history for the inspiration for this pattern. James Henshall developed a similar pattern for bass over a hundred years ago, but it was tied with shorter, stiffer hackles. "They didn't have grizzly hackles back then," Petrie pointed out. His original Roadkill pattern, developed for Orvis Houston well over ten years ago, was unweighted. Petrie now favors adding bead chain eyes to give it some weight, a further evolution of the pattern. His reason: Fish will often pass up a pattern presented above them, but will hit a fly that is the same depth or deeper than they are. A weighted fly will therefore sink down into the strike zone. "I guess that shows my changing taste in fly-fishing," he said. "Several years ago, I would have never fished with a weighted fly."

Petrie fishes the Bead Eye Roadkill all year long, noting the fish like it regardless of the season. When blind-casting in deeper water, Petrie suggested using what he called a "searching strip." The idea is to cover a lot of water and find the fish. Long strips cause the splayed hackles to undulate in the water.

The Bead Eye Roadkill is also a heck of a sight-casting pattern. The weighted eyes allow it to be fished on the bottom like a crab pattern. "Those long hackles wave around in the water and really create a lot of movement, even in tall grass." said Petrie.

TYING INSTRUCTIONS

STEP 1 Tie eye-to-bend thread base. Tie four, 3-inch grizzly saddle hackles as shown. Add 4 strands Krystal Flash and Flashabou each side of tail.

STEP 2 Tie 2 long, webby hackles above barb.

STEP 3 Palmer hackles forward to just behind hook eye, leaving space for eyes.

STEP 4 Tie Krystal Flash and Flashabou at head, placing around shank to cover body. Figure-8 wrap eyes as shown, tie off, whip finish.

VARIATIONS

The Bead Eye Roadkill can be tied with yellow, red, chartreuse, orange, or natural grizzly hackles.

Big-B

BRIAN HANDLIN

MATERIALS:

Hook:	Mustad 34011, No. 2-2/0
Thread:	Chartreuse or clear monofilament
Tail:	Bucktail, white Krystal Flash, pearl
Eyes:	Painted lead dumbbell eyes
Body:	Cactus Chenille, chartreuse

IN A PREVIOUS LIFE, HONORARY TEXAN BRIAN HANDLIN managed an outfitters store in the Florida Keys. One day, a good friend dropped by the store seeking a pattern similar to the bucktail jigs he used successfully for Spanish mackerel.

Brian's friend, Captain Jack Callion, was guiding Mark Sosin that week as they filmed a segment of "Saltwater Journal." Callion returned the next evening with Sosin in tow. The little bucktail pattern Handlin created was a definite hit with the fish. Sosin gushed that it was the best day of mackerel fishing he had ever enjoyed. When the television personality inquired about the pattern's name, Handlin responded that he never named his patterns, and that Sosin could call it anything he chose. Sosin and Callion conferred, and the pattern acquired Handlin's nickname with the guides in the area, "Big-B."

Sosin has featured the Big-B on three different segments of his television show, and told Handlin on a follow-up trip several years later that he has caught just about every species of inshore fish on the fly.

Handlin, who moved to Texas to manage the fly shop for Bass Pro Shops in Katy, finds the Big-B works just as well in Texas waters. One day last summer, he caught and released nearly 50 speckled trout while blind-casting the surf at San Louis Pass. He uses the Big-B in any situation where he would use a jig.

Handlin fishes the Big-B with short, fast, erratic strips. The fly is tied on the back of the hook to minimize the need for a wire bite tippet. Wire can be added, but Handlin noted that it should be short, no longer than 3 inches.

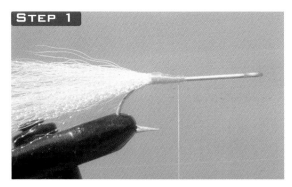

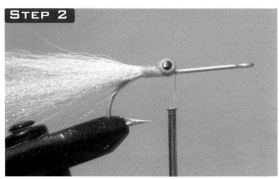

TYING INSTRUCTIONS

STEP 1 Lay thread base from ½-inch ahead of hook point to bend. Tie hook-length bucktail bundle near bend. Add 5-6 strands Krystal Flash either side of tail.

STEP 2 Figure-8 wrap eyes on thread base ahead of tail.

STEP 3 Tie Cactus Chenille ahead of eyes, wrap back to tail. Figure-8 chenille around eyes, tie off just ahead of eyes. Whip finish, Zap-A-Gap thread wraps.

VARIATIONS

A VMC trailer hook used on spinnerbaits can be substituted for the Mustad 34011. Body and eyes can be any color.

Butt Ugly

HERB MOSMAN

MATERIALS:

Hooks:	Tiemco 811S, No. 4-6 Tiemco, 9394, No. 6
Thread:	Ultra Size 140, brown
Eyes:	1/36-ounce dumbbell eyes, painted red with black pupil
Hinge:	Guitar string, number 9
Body:	African goat hair, fiery brown Antron fibers, gold
Legs:	Sili Legs, pumpkin/GR-OR-black flake
Glue:	Zap-A-Gap Dubbing wax

HERB MOSMAN HAS SPENT MOST OF HIS LIFE THROWING flies in his native Colorado. After sampling several of our mild Texas winters, he and his wife moved to San Antonio. It wasn't long before this life-long fly-fisherman was sight-casting on the middle coast and tinkering with new saltwater patterns.

One of Mosman's creations is the Butt Ugly. Sometimes called a hinge fly or wiggle fly, the humble Mosman is quick to point out that his pattern isn't really new, but a new twist. "Hinge flies have been around for years," he said. "I just adapted it for use in saltwater. To get the fly down on the bottom, I added lead eyes. In addition, I experimented with the placement of the legs."

A trip to the coast convinced Mosman that the Butt Ugly was something special. While wading across a shallow grass flat, he caught and released 15 large black drum. "Redfish like it too," he said.

Mosman said there are two main reasons why the Butt Ugly is so productive. "Many Texas anglers have a fondness for chartreuse and white patterns," he said. "I think fish strike some patterns just because they look different. Plus, the Butt Ugly looks like a fleeing crab on the bottom."

Mosman noted that African goat hair is a great material for saltwater patterns, but can be hard to dub. To make it easier to work with, he mixed the goat hair with small bits of Antron fibers. The Antron also gives the dubbed body a little sparkle.

The fly's heavy lead eyes make it a challenge to cast, but Mosman stressed that the results were worth the effort. Mosman suggested casting the Butt Ugly in front of cruising fish and allowing it to settle to the bottom. Then impart a short series of 6- to 8-inch strips so the fish notices the movement. Stop stripping when the fish rushes it. Mosman noted that fish are not bashful about taking the fly, and very few will study it before striking.

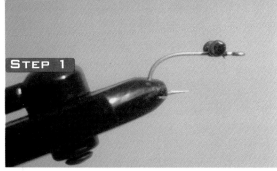

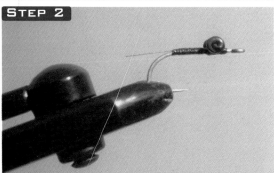

Because the fly is heavily weighted, it is also effective for fishing deep drop-offs and channels during the winter.

TYING INSTRUCTIONS

STEP 1 Figure-8 wrap eyes as shown on 811S hook, leaving room for dubbing and rubber legs.

STEP 2 Tie ¾-inch guitar string as shown. Zap-A-Gap wraps, let dry.

STEP 3 Mount 9394 hook in vise, start thread above hook point. Mix Antron fibers with goat hair to root beer color. Zap-A-Gap thread, apply fiber mixture. Dub forward within ¼ inch of eye. Tie legs, leaving them no shorter than ¾ inch, angling down back. Complete dubbing to eye, tie off, whip finish.

STEP 4 (Vise not needed for this step. Photo shows detail of finished tail section.) Cut hook where dubbing stops.

STEP 5 Attach hinged body, passing guitar string through eye of tail section and bending guitar string into loop. Tie end of guitar string, Zap-A-Gap wraps. If hinged does not move freely, enlarge loop with dubbing needle.

STEP 6 Dubbing forward, complete front section creating tapered body. Figure-8 wrap over and around eyes. Tie legs underneath eyes, positioning down and back as shown. Complete dubbing ahead of eyes, tie off, whip finish.

VARIATIONS

The Butt Ugly can be tied with a variety of eyes, ranging from large lead dumbbells for fishing deep water to bead chain eyes for shallower areas.

De-Bonaire

CAPTAIN STEVE SOULÉ

MATERIALS:

Hook:	Mustad 34007, No. 4, 6 or 8
Thread:	Waxed Danville Flymaster Plus, size A, dark tan
Eyes:	Unpainted dumbbell, extra small
Flash:	Krystal Flash, rootbeer
Tail:	White grizzly hackle tips
Collar:	Saddle hackles, white
Coating:	Loon Hard Head, chartreuse and clear

CAPTAIN STEVE SOULÉ SPENT PART OF HIS YOUTH IN south Florida. Bonefish, tarpon, and snook were his "Big Three" back then. Soulé's uncle, a professional fishing guide in the Keys, helped impart fly-fishing knowledge, rapidly accelerating the learning curve.

Soulé's first saltwater patterns were specifically designed for fishing the Florida flats. When this Austin native moved back to Texas, he found that his patterns fooled flats dwellers in the Lone Star State just as well as they did in Florida.

The De-Bonaire (pronounced "deh bone air") is one of Soulé's go-to bonefish patterns. He found that redfish like it just as much as silver ghosts do.

"I like to throw the De-Bonaire on light-wind days when I need a delicate presentation," he said. "I originally tied it on a number 6 or 8 hook, but I now tie it on a number 4 hook for redfish."

The De-Bonaire is designed to ride hook-point-up. Because the fly has small eyes and a palmered hackle, it does not sink fast.

Soulé suggested tying the De-Bonaire in shades of tan or olive when fishing over grass beds. "I try to make it appear as something natural," he said.

Soulé likes to cast close to a cruising or tailing fish and retrieve with short, quick strips after the fly reaches depth. Strips should be no longer than 4-6 inches, sometimes as short as 2 inches.

Soulé also noted that the De-Bonaire is a great prospecting fly for blind-casting to potholes.

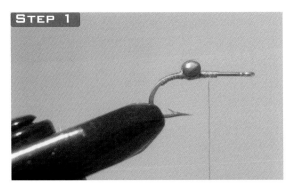

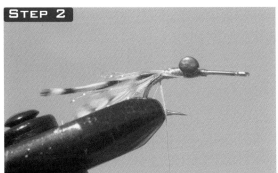

Tying Instructions

STEP 1 Tie thread halfway between eye and bend. Tie eyes directly over hook point as shown.

STEP 2 Tie 8 strands Krystal Flash behind eyes, wrap slightly on bend. Tie 2 hackle feathers splayed slightly outward on either side.

STEP 3 Tie 2 hackle feathers near bend, palmer forward, tie off just behind eyes. Build thread body tapering down to hook eye, whip finish.

STEP 4 Paint eye tips chartreuse, clear coat body.

Dr. Ed's Redfish Special

DR. ED RIZZOLO

MATERIALS:

Hook:	Mustad 34011, No. 4 or 6
Thread:	3/0 Monocord, black or orange
Eyes:	Medium bead chain, silver, gold or brass
Tail:	Marabou, short orange feathers
Body:	Flat Mylar tinsel, gold V Rib, clear or Body Lace
Underwing:	Fox squirrel tail Krystal Flash, gold
Overwing:	Grizzly hackle feathers, neck or saddle

*MANY OF THE FEATURED FLY-TIERS IN THIS BOOK WERE FLY-*fishing pioneers on the Texas coast. Although most have 10-20 years experience, I was not able to find anyone who has been fly-fishing the salt longer than Dr. Ed Rizzolo, whom I consider the dean of saltwater fly-fishing in the state.

Rizzolo started tying flies back in 1944, a year before he learned to fly-fish. Growing up in the northeastern United States, he primarily fished regional trout streams. He came to Texas in 1950 to attend graduate school. He entered medical school in 1952, the same year he started fly-fishing the Texas coast.

"Back then, saltwater flies were nothing more than a clump of bucktail tied on a hook," he said. "Now, patterns are much more creative."

Rizzolo considers his pattern a "composite fly."

"It really doesn't look like anything in particular," he said. "Each individual component was chosen because it was appealing to a redfish."

Rizzolo felt the significant components were the gold body, the orange wing and also the eyes. He felt strongly that eyes are absolutely necessary for a pattern to be successful in saltwater.

The Redfish Special is tied very sparsely, which makes for easy casting in stiff coastal breezes. "I guess tying sparsely dressed flies comes from my roots as a Catskills fly-tier," Rizzolo said. "I always thought a fly with less dressing will behave better in the water."

"I experiment with a new pattern in a tank of water. I check the sink rate, then adjust the amount of material in the wing and tail until I get the desired performance."

To check the Redfish Special's effectiveness, Rizzolo tied a bunch and gave them to friends with penchants

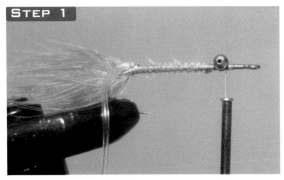

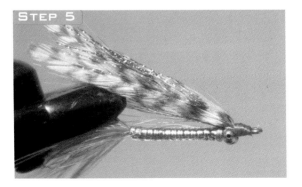

for redfish. All the reports came back very positive. One such report came from Chico Fernandez, whom Rizzolo met years before at a tying conclave.

Rizzolo fishes his pattern quite a few different ways. In shallow water, he swims the fly using very long strips. Over sand and mud, he hops it along the bottom. Regardless of location, he suggested varying the retrieve until you find something the fish like.

TYING INSTRUCTIONS

STEP 1 De-barb and sharpen hook. Lay bend-to-eye thread base. Tie eyes ³/₁₆ inch behind hook eye. Tie marabou feathers behind eyes, wrapping evenly to tail and extending ½ inch beyond bend as shown. Tie V Rib just ahead of tail, wrap thread forward to eye.

STEP 2 Tie tinsel behind eyes, wrap to tail, then forward to eyes, tie off.

STEP 3 Wrap V Rib forward over body to eyes, tie off. Stretching while winding gives segmented appearance.

STEP 4 Rotate vise, hook point up. Tie sparse squirrel tail bundle just ahead of eyes. Add 8 strands Krystal Flash atop squirrel tail. Both materials extend ½ inch beyond bend.

STEP 5 Tie 2 grizzly hackles flared outward as shown. Wind tapered head, tie off.

VARIATIONS

This pattern should be tied with light bead chain eyes when fishing in water less than 2 feet. For deeper water, substitute heavier eyes.

Laguna Critter

CAPTAIN JON FAILS

MATERIALS:

Hook:	Tiemco TMC 800S, Size 8 or TMC 811S, Size 6
Thread:	6/0 Uni-Thread, tan, camel or rusty brown
Weedguard:	15-pound Hard Mason (optional)
Palps:	Bucktail, White and two grizzly hackle tips
Eyes:	Black plastic seed beads on 25-pound mono. Cover beads with clear head cement
Antennae:	PolarFlash, Pink Peal and Krystal Flash
Body:	Medium chenille and 2-3 duck flank feathers (widgeon, redhead or pintail)
Legs:	Palmer wound hackle feathers
Coating:	Clear nail polish

CAPTAIN JON FAILS, A LIGHT TACKLE SPECIALIST, PLIES the rich waters of Laguna Madre. Whether his clients are fishing with conventional tackle or a fly rod, sight-casting is the name of the game.

Corpus Christi serves as Fails' home base. Chicago may have gotten the moniker "Windy City," but Corpus has the wind, averaging over 20 mph daily. The breezes of the coastal bend have humbled more than a few good fly-fishermen.

Fails is extremely sensitive about the wind resistance of the flies he chooses. "A pattern is of no use if you can't get it close enough for the fish to see it," he said.

The Laguna Critter is one of Fails' pet patterns he has developed over several years of guiding. "My clients were having problems with grass fouling Clouser Minnows in shallow water," he explained. "On top of that, the fish were turning up their noses at bendback patterns. A topwater would have worked great, but hair bugs are just too hard to throw in our wind. I wanted a pattern that would float or suspend over the grass beds, make an extremely soft presentation, and look like a shrimp or crab."

Borrowing a few dry fly concepts, Fails incorporated a large, webby hackle into the Laguna Critter, which allows it to float when dry and sink slowly when saturated. The hackle allows the pattern to land as softly as a dandelion bloom.

Fails coaches his clients to throw the little fly directly at a tailing fish. "If a redfish sees the pattern or senses it's movement, you will see the tail go under," he explained. "Strip once and you usually get a strike."

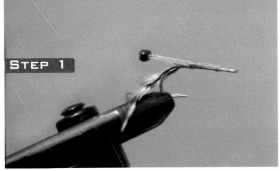

Somewhat sheepishly, Fails admitted that some of his fly-fishing clients are less than stellar casters. When a client can't seem to hit the broad side of a barn, Fails puts them casting to sand pockets in grass beds. "Allow the Laguna Critter to fall to the bottom then slowly crawl it across the sand like a small crab," he instructs them. "Because the Laguna Critter looks like several different types of bait, you do not have to move it for it to be effective.

"And just because I may have a client cast to some potholes, it doesn't mean I think they are a bad caster." Fails chuckled.

TYING INSTRUCTIONS

STEP 1 Tie 2 grizzly hackle tips 45 degrees to shank, splay slightly outward shiny sides up. Tie eyes angled slightly up and out.

STEP 2 Tie white bucktail from head as shown. Add several strands Krystal Flash, 4-6 strands pink pearl Polar Flash.

STEP 3 Tie chenille near eyes, wrap forward to eye, tie off. Tie hackle butt near eyes base palmer forward, tie off.

STEP 4 Trim top off palmered hackle.

STEP 5 Cement trimmed portion (cement or nail polish), wait until tacky. Cement flank feathers' undersides, tie by the stem near hook eye.

STEP 6 Cement feathers to sides, mold to shape, let dry. Trim barbules (legs) to shape.

VARIATIONS

The Laguna Critter can be tied without the duck feather carapace.

Patrick's 20/20

PATRICK ELKINS

MATERIALS:

Hook:	Mustad 34007, No. 2-4
Thread:	Tan Fly Master Plus or 3/0
Eyes:	Bead chain, gold medium size
Epoxy Eyes:	30 pound Climax Saltwater monofilament 2 hour epoxy (5 min. epoxy will work but it is harder to work with) Midge (15/0) black (#033) Killer Cad dis Glass Beads Small (11/0) Gold (#085) Killer Cad dis Glass Beads Small (11/) Amber (#069) Killer Cad dis Glass Beads Medium-stiff mono leader (approx. 20-30 lb.) Black felt-tip pen
Body:	Estaz or Ice Chenille, root beer
Legs:	Webby saddle hackle, brown or grizzly
Wing:	Fly Fur, tan
Marker:	Permanent marker, brown or black

ONE DAY OVER LUNCH, PATRICK ELKINS HELD FORTH ABOUT how shrimp react when trying to escape a predator. "Unlike baitfish that look forward while fleeing, shrimp look backward at their pursuers," he said. "Their head and large eyes make a prominent target. Most fly-tiers concentrate on the profile of a shrimp, but fish key in on their head and eyes." Pointing the hook end of a fly at me, Elkins asked, "From that direction, doesn't that look just like a shrimp's head?"

The aft end of Patrick's 20/20 does, indeed, look like the head of a fleeing shrimp. The epoxy eyes really stand out while the Fly Fur creates the perfect illusion of a rostrum, but the body is crab-like in appearance. Elkins said the fly is really an attractor pattern because it reflects characteristics of both crabs and shrimp.

Elkins pointed out several differences between shrimp and crabs. Crabs do not move at a particularly fast rate, while shrimp do. In addition, crabs move in a straight line while shrimp hop around quickly and randomly. These are key points to remember when working the Patrick's 20/20. "If there is an abundance of shrimp in the area, fish the pattern as if it were a shrimp," he said. "If crabs seem to be the food source of the day, strip the fly to simulate a crab."

Because the pattern looks like both food sources, Elkins sometimes employs a retrieve that simulates both crab and a shrimp. "Cast the fly 3-5 feet in front of the fish and give a couple of short, aggressive strips like a shrimp would act," he said. "The movement will get the fish's attention. As soon as the fish sees the fly and turns towards it, drop let it settle to the bottom. As the fish gets right up to the fly to give it a sniff, give the fly a long,

slow strip like a crab would act. Then get ready to hit him hard because once the fish sees those epoxy eyes, it's all over."

INSTRUCTIONS FOR MAKING EYES (NOT SHOWN)

STEP 1 Slightly melt one end of 3-inch piece 30-pound mono. While molten, tap end to flatten to slightly larger diameter than bead hole. Color black with felt pen.

STEP 2 Slide 1 black, 1 gold, and 1 amber bead (in order) onto the mono to the flattened eye.

STEP 3 Epoxy beads, rotate until dry.

STEP 4 Cut off 1½ inches of excess mono, add beads in reverse order, melt and flatten mono, color end with marker, epoxy and rotate until dry. Bend mono to 45 degrees.

TYING INSTRUCTIONS

STEP 1 Tie bead eyes above hook point.

STEP 2 Tie tan Fly Fur behind eyes extending 1-1½ inches past front of hook, wrap slightly toward bend.

STEP 3 Tie 5-inch piece Estaz or Ice Chenille atop Fly Fur.

STEP 4 Tie 1 long grizzly hackle atop Estaz and Fly Fur.

STEP 5 Figure-8 wrap epoxy eyes behind bead eyes, angled down 20 degrees from shank. Superglue wraps.

STEP 6 Advance thread back to hook eye. Wrap Estaz forward to hook eye, figure-8 wrap around epoxy eyes, tie off. Wrap hackle in same way, tie off at hook eye. Trim Estaz and hackle. With a permanent marker, add evenly spaced hash marks on Fly Fur.

Redfish Nymph

CAPTAIN SCOTT SOMMERLATTE

MATERIALS:

Hook:	Tiemco 800s, No. 2
Thread:	Flymaster Plus, white
Eyes:	EyeBalz
Body:	Grizzly hackles (from a number 2 neck) Salmon colored hackles
Tail:	Grizzly Hackles (from a number 2 neck)
Weedguard:	40-lb. Climax mono (optional)

SELF-PROCLAIMED "FISHING NOMAD" CAPTAIN SCOTT Sommerlatte makes annual junkets with clients to the Florida Keys, Lower Laguna Madre, and all points in between. Sommerlatte also spends significant time each year plying the waters of Port O'Connor. It was here that he developed the Redfish Nymph for winter redfish.

To most fly-fishermen, nymphing and saltwater fly-fishing are mutually exclusive terms. Nonetheless, Sommerlatte said he routinely catches fish during the winter using this technique.

Beginning in late autumn and extending through late spring, cold fronts regularly push through to the coast causing water temperatures to drop. Bright sunshine after a front quickly warms the shallows. During a falling tide, sun-warmed water pours off the flats and into guts and drains, creating small saltwater tributaries. In turn, predators stack up in these warm areas and wait for the groceries to sweep by.

Realizing that standard sight-casting patterns are not designed for swift currents, Sommerlatte set out to find a solution. He reasoned that a successful offering must incorporate several important features. First, the fly must be able to get down quickly. Second, it must push a lot of water to attract attention. And last, it should be brightly colored for turbid conditions.

Like experimental aircraft, new patterns evolve over time. Even the name is subject to change. Sommerlatte tenderly refers to each of his new creations as the Matagorda Hoochie Mama. Only after a new fly has proven itself in the salt will it be given a formal name. After several successful winter trips, the Redfish Nymph was officially christened.

Like its freshwater counterparts, the Redfish Nymph was designed to be fished in a current. If you are fishing from a boat, position yourself to cast directly upcurrent. Allow the fly to tumble back in the current, stripping in line as needed. If you are wading, stand on the edge of the gut and cast up- and crosscurrent, mending line as

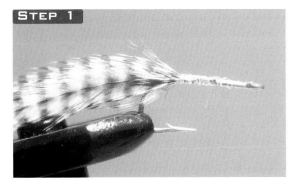

needed.

Sommerlatte noted that you should set the hook if the fly line stops or hesitates during the drift.

TYING INSTRUCTIONS

STEP 1 Tie 4 grizzly hackles for tail.

STEP 2 Tie 2 grizzly hackles at base and palmer forward to create collar covering ⅔ of shank.

STEP 3 Tie 2 salmon hackles near hook eye. Tie EyeBalz atop hackles.

STEP 4 Figure-8 wrap salmon hackles on shank, palmer back to bend. Grizzly and salmon hackles should meet.

STEP 5 Bend 40-pound mono into weedguard, tie near hook eye.

CHAPTER 6
Drum & Sheepshead Patterns

Green Weenie

LES LEHMAN, JR.

MATERIALS:

Hook:	Mustad 34007, No. 6 or 8
Thread:	Black
Eyes:	Medium bead chain, gold
Body:	Rabbit dubbing Flashabou dubbing, pearl
Hackle:	Grizzly saddle hackle, olive

SPEND TIME WADING SHIN-DEEP FLATS IN SEARCH OF REDFISH and you are bound to see a convict or two. Convict fish, that is. Given their black and white barred color scheme, it is easy to see how sheepshead acquired their unusual nickname.

During a conversation with Les Lehman, Jr., he highlighted the large amount of sheepshead that frequent the flats. "Especially during the late spring, the water is still too cold for redfish, but there will be sheepshead everywhere," he said.

Sheepshead have a reputation as one of the toughest fish to catch on a fly, so much so they are sometimes referred to as "Texas permit."

"Because of their wide profile, they are great sport to catch on a fly rod," noted Lehman. "But I had never heard of anyone catching them consistently, so I wanted a fly to target them."

Through trial and error, Lehman came up with what may be the only pattern ever developed strictly for sheepshead. And so it was that the Green Weenie came about.

Lehman realized he was onto something when he and a friend caught and released 30 sheepshead on a weekend fishing trip. Other anglers whispered their praise of the Green Weenie to me, as if the pattern were some great secret that might leak out.

Sheepshead are equipped with some interesting dental work. A set of incisor teeth, remarkably like those of a sheep, gives the fish its name. Further back in the mouth is a set of "molars," rows of hard plates to grind up barnacles, shell, and crabs.

Getting a solid hookset on a sheepshead is a challenge in itself, the barb easily deflected by the bony mouth parts. "To get more purchase, I widened the gap of the hook," Lehman said. "Although I still miss lots of fish, this has significantly improved my hookup rate.

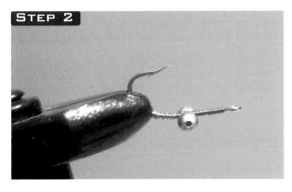

"The Green Weenie must look like some sort of benthic worm. You need to fish it over hard sand or the fish will never find it. A long leader is essential for catching sheepshead on the flats. I fish with a 15-foot leader, the last three feet 6- or 8-pound-test fluorocarbon to help reduce visibility."

Lehman likes to cast the Green Weenie 10-20 feet in front of a fish and strip it several times. If the fish sees the fly, it will rush it. If the fish ignores the pattern, Lehman picks it up and casts again. "You will spook a sheepshead if you cast within 10 feet of it," he said. "Once the fish darts to the fly, it will usually tail on it. It is important to set the hook only after the fish stops tailing and starts to swim away. Even then, you will sometimes pull it out of their mouth. I have had some fish tail on the fly five or six times. For some reason, this fly really gets the fish worked up."

TYING INSTRUCTIONS

STEP 1 (Not shown) Slightly widen hook gap.

STEP 2 Attach eyes mid-shank. Wind thread to rear of hook.

STEP 3 Tie grizzly hackle butt at bend.

STEP 4 Mix rabbit fur and Flashabou dubbing. Wax several inches thread, apply rabbit fur/Flashabou, create double-tapered body.

STEP 5 Palmer hackle forward to hook eye with hackle pliers, tie off.

STEP 6 Trim bottom hackle close to body. Trim top hackle even with hook point.

Drum Beat

CAPTAIN DANNO WISE

MATERIALS:

Hook:	Mustad 34011, Size 6 or 8
Thread:	6/0, Black
Tail:	Crosscut rabbit fur, black
Eyes:	Silver bead chain, medium
Body:	Black chenille
Wing:	Crosscut rabbit fur, black

LIKE MANY TEXAS FLATS FISHERMEN, CAPTAIN DANNO WISE took note of the large number of puppy drum and sheepshead he saw while stalking trout and redfish. Not knowing of a fly that would fool these flats inhabitants, he set out to find a pattern to throw when the opportunity presented itself.

"The Drum Beat must represent some type of sand worm," Wise said. "Dark, solid colors seem to work the best."

While developing the pattern, he experimented with different types of flashy material only to find that it spooked the fish. He cautioned against using any flash in a pattern if drum are the target.

"I wanted something with a lot of action, even when I wasn't stripping," he said. "That is why I chose rabbit fur. I think it has even more action in the water than marabou."

Wise uses what he calls a "dead retrieve" when fishing the Drum Beat. With the fly on the bottom, he makes several 2-inch strips then stops. "I want the fly to appear to be something burrowing in the sand," he explained. "Basically, something that looks like an easy meal.

"Murky water is your friend when fishing for drum and sheepshead. Your casts don't need to be as long and you can afford to be sloppier."

Wise brought up an interesting paradox that may explain why sheepshead are so difficult to catch on a fly.

"Most fish are predators prone to impulse strikes, but sheepshead are scavengers and so do not instinctively strike. That gives them additional time to visually inspect an offering."

Wise said drum and sheepshead gently inhale the fly then slowly move off. "You may not be able to see the strike or feel it when it happens," he said. "Once the fish moves off, the pressure on the fly line lets you know it is time to set the hook."

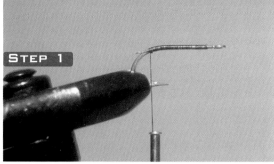

STEP 1

STEP 2

STEP 3

STEP 4

STEP 5

STEP 6

TYING INSTRUCTIONS

STEP 1 Lay eye-to-bend thread base.

STEP 2 Tie in rabbit fur bundle at bend.

STEP 3 Tie eyes atop rabbit fur.

STEP 4 Tie chenille ahead of eyes.

STEP 5 Wrap chenille forward to eye, tie off.

STEP 6 Tie in second bunch of rabbit fur behind eye, whip finish.

VARIATIONS

The Drum Beat can also be tied in solid olive or brown.

The Little Black Fly

COREY RICH

MATERIALS:

Hook:	Mustad 34007, No. 4
Thread:	Size 3, A or 6, black
Body:	Small or medium chenille, black .015 diameter lead wire (optional)
Underwing:	Bucktail, black Krystal Flash, black
Overwing:	Barred grizzly hackles

"CAPTAIN CHUCK SCATES GAVE A PRESENTATION TO OUR fly-fishing club several years ago about fly-fishing for black drum," said Corey Rich. "Chuck discussed how challenging they are to take on a fly rod, and suggested that small, dark flies work the best."

"The first time I cast The Little Black Fly to a drum, it ate it. The next time I cast to a drum, it was nudged out of the way by a redfish that grabbed the fly. At that point, I thought I might be onto something."

Rather than include his name in the fly's moniker, Rich simply called it The Little Black Fly. "It's too general a pattern to claim that I did anything special," he said. "I started with a bendback pattern tied on a No. 4 hook and went from there."

The Little Black Fly is now his go-to pattern when surrounded by drum on the flats. "I am not sure why they like it, but I have a hunch it represents some type of benthic worm," Rich said.

Rich often cruises the flats in his kayak, which allows him to cover a lot of water. "You can tell where drum have been feeding because the bottom will be pockmarked," he explained. Called "blowholes" by Rich, he suggested committing these areas to memory because drum will often return to the same areas again and again.

Rich often finds blowholes in muddy areas between a line of spartina grass and a sea grass bed. "They seem to like those areas quite a bit," he said.

As of this writing, Rich's biggest black drum on The Little Black Fly taped 25 inches, a hefty prize on a fly rod by anyone's standards. He prefers fishing the pattern over mud bottoms.

Two friends, Jerry Loring and Fred Carr, suggested that he add a bit of contrasting color to the fly. To keep the color combinations straight, Rich established a naming convention: A fly with a chartreuse chenille butt section added to the black body is a "Firefly." A hot pink butt section becomes a "Firetail."

When sight-casting to black drum, Rich likes to cast directly at a fish. "Let the fly settle, then give it the slight-

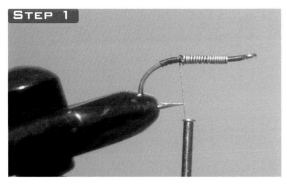

est twitch," he said. "At that point, the fish will either eat it or turn away. If it turns away or appears disinterested, pick up and cast again.

"For redfish, I cast in front of a tailing or cruising fish and retrieve in short strips."

TYING INSTRUCTIONS

STEP 1 Slightly bend hook eye away from barb. Lay down eye-to-shank thread base. Wrap 10 turns lead wire, ending ¼ inch from hook eye. Overwrap wire with several turns thread, ending at bend.

STEP 2 Tie chenille near bend, wrap forward just past wire but short of eye.

STEP 3 Rotate vise, hook point up. Tie sparse bucktail tuft behind eye.

STEP 4 Add 6 strands Krystal Flash atop wing.

STEP 5 Tie in 2 grizzly hackles as overwing. Whip finish, cement head.

VARIATIONS

The Little Black Fly can be tied with a contrasting colored butt section. Chartreuse and hot pink are popular choices.

CHAPTER 7
Poppers

Danno's Popping Shrimp

CAPTAIN DANNO WISE

MATERIALS:

Hook:	Mustad 34011, No. 4
Thread:	6/0, white
Antennae:	Bucktail
Eyes:	Monofilament
Body:	Ice Chenille Live Body foam, rectangle – cut to shape

"A PANICKED SHRIMP WILL SKIP ACROSS THE WATER'S surface trying desperately to escape" said Captain Danno Wise. "I had seen all types of poppers that imitated a fleeing baitfish, but never a fleeing shrimp. That's why I decided to develop this pattern."

Danno's Popping Shrimp provides a large silhouette in the water, yet is easy to cast. The innovative pattern is a beginning fly-tier's dream--cheap, durable, and quick to tie. Best of all, the fish like it.

The popper's construction makes it highly versatile. "Depending on style of retrieve, you can chug it with a quick snap of the wrist, or make it gurgle and crawl across the water," Wise said. "And because the body is made of foam, you can make a very quiet presentation in shallow water."

Having spent a number of years guiding fly-fishing clients on the lower Texas coast, Wise developed quite a few interesting tricks and techniques. Wise and his wife, Marisa, now hold fly-fishing schools along the Texas coast where they share that knowledge.

"From a guide's perspective, you have to be able to see your client's fly in the water, and it's relation to the fish you are casting to," Wise said. "I coach my clients when to strip, when to pause, and when to make another cast. You can't do that if you can't see the fly."

The upturned rostrum on Danno's Popping Shrimp is a clever innovation that makes the fly easy to see by both guide and client. "That little triangle that sticks up on the head can be seen for a long way," he said. "I find that clients can see this fly much better than other patterns."

Wise said redfish and trout readily eat the fly when fished over shallow grass flats. "My favorite retrieve is to strip it quickly so skips across the surface," he said. "That drives fish nuts. If the fish are skittish, I switch to a slow retrieve using short strips. This fly works well for blind-casting, too."

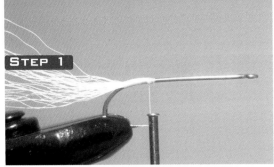

TYING INSTRUCTIONS

STEP 1 Tie bucktail at bend.

STEP 2 Tie eyes atop bucktail

STEP 3 Tie chenille strand near bend, ahead of eyes

STEP 4 Cut foam body to shape. (It is better to make the body longer than you need and do a final trim.) Make two chenille wraps, tie down foam, positioning shrimp's horn directly over bend.

STEP 5 Wrap thread forward, wrap chenille to hook eye, tie off.

STEP 6 Tie off foam near eye, extending ⅛ inch beyond eye, whip finish.

VARIATIONS

Danno's Popping Shrimp can be tied with a brown, chartreuse, or pink body.

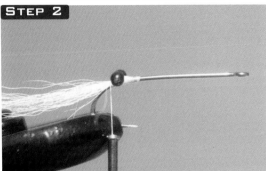

East Cut Redfish Popper

T.J. NEAL

MATERIALS:

Hook:	Mustad 34007, No. 6
Thread:	Size A Danville Flymaster Plus, any color
Body:	Wapsi hard Styrofoam popper body, size 8
Tail:	Krystal Flash, red
Paint:	Testors model paint, flat red
Eyes:	Prismatic stick-on eyes
Glitter:	Fine red glitter
Glue:	Flex Coat rod finishing epoxy

SMALL POPPERS ARE A GREAT CHOICE WHEN SIGHT-CASTING or blind-casting a promising flat. Their small, cupped faces kick up just the right amount of water to get a fish's attention.

T. J. Neal's company produces mass quantities of East Cut Poppers for the Texas market. Neal admitted that the little popper isn't much different than other poppers, but he pointed out several features he incorporated into this pattern. "The glitter on the back adds a lot of sparkle to the fly," he said. "In addition, the tail is made with Krystal Flash, which is something I had never seen before."

Neal likes to use several light coats of epoxy to form a rock-hard shell on top of the paint. "I have seen friends errantly bounce the fly off pilings and exposed oyster shell while fishing," he said with a laugh. "Two light coats of epoxy keeps the finish very nice, even if you have a few mishaps."

When targeting tailing or backing redfish, Neal suggested casting as close to the fish as you can and stripping very slowly. "Pretend you are trying to sneak the fly away from the fish," Neal advised. "When retrieved this way, the little popper wiggles back and forth in the water. It drives the fish nuts."

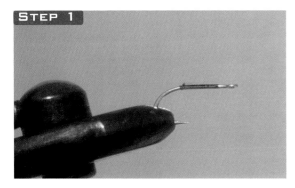

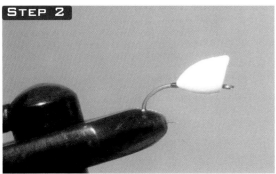

TYING INSTRUCTIONS

STEP 1 Wrap eye-to-bend thread base.

STEP 2 Seat popper body on thread base.

STEP 3 Tie ½-inch bunch Krystal Flash to form tail (popper body removed in photo to show detail).

STEP 4 Paint popper body desired color, leaving mouth unpainted, let dry. (Optionally, paint hook eye.) Add stick-on eyes, fronts touch mold line line in popper body.

STEP 5 Epoxy body, careful to completely fill underside gap and cover tail wraps. (Avoid using too much epoxy, it adds a lot of weight.) Sprinkle back with glitter, rotate until dry 45 minutes to an hour on drying wheel. Apply second epoxy coat to back and bottom. (It is not necessary to recoat the mouth

VARIATIONS

The East Cut Redfish Popper can be tied in a variety of colors. Chartreuse, copper, and red/white are very productive.

CHAPTER 8
Sliders & Divers

Bill's Redneck Slider

BILL TRUSSELL

MATERIALS:

Hook:	Tiemco 811S or Mustad 34007, No. 4 or 6
Thread:	Single strand tying floss or your favorite hair spinning thread
Tail:	Bucktail, red Krystal Flash Bucktail, chartreuse
Body:	Deer body hair, red Deer body hair, chartreuse
Eyes:	Medium or large doll eyes, red or yellow
Glue:	Goop Zap-a-Gap
Nail polish:	Clear (Optional)
Floatant:	Watershed or equivalent

FLY-FISHING AND SIGHT-CASTING ARE SYNONYMOUS TO BILL Trussell. He is often seen wading the shallows of the upper coast with a fly rod in one hand and a deer-hair fly in the other, ready to cast the instant he spies a cruising redfish.

Trussell shared an anecdote from a presentation to his fly-fishing club by Captain Chris Phillips. Phillips drew a parallel between sight-casting to redfish and bowhunting for deer: You are not sitting in a blind, you are out stalking your prey. When it is crunch time, you better make your first shot count. "I can't describe it any better than that." Trussell said.

Trussell is a well-known fly-tier in the Houston area, and has a distinct fondness for spinning deer hair. "I really like fishing with deer-hair bugs, but they can be awfully wind resistant," he said. "When I developed this pattern, I needed something that would cast easily and kiss the water like a butterfly's wing."

The Redneck Slider is a very productive pattern that is sold in many fly shops across the state. Smaller in diameter than a nickel, the little slider is a joy to cast. Its quiet entry is a major advantage when stealth is required. "The Redneck Slider lands much more quietly than a hard bodied popper," Trussell said. "Plus, fish seem to hang onto deer hair patterns longer than they do hard poppers."

Trussell said the Redneck Slider is very versatile fly that can be popped to get a fish's attention, pulled under water, or dragged across the surface. "Coating the flat underside with fingernail polish helps reduce the water resistance," he said.

Once he casts to a cruising or tailing fish, Trussell likes to give the slider 3-5 quick strips to get the fish's attention. "If the fish turns, continue inching the fly forward until the fish eats it," he said.

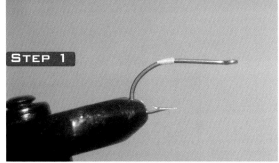

TYING INSTRUCTIONS

STEP 1 Lay narrow floss base above point and barb, tie off.

STEP 2 Tie small bucktail bundle cut from the base (base hair is more hollow and flares better) on thread base, evening tips. Topmost strands flare from shank 45 degrees, extending 1½ inches beyond bend. Tie 10-15 strands Krystal Flash, trim equal to bucktail. Make several wraps around bucktail, creating even taper, tie down. Zap-A-Gap windings, let dry.

STEP 3 Cut thick red body hair bundle, brush away underfur, even the tips. Trim butts to make bundle 1½ inches. Next spin the hair by holding bundle against shank, make two loose wraps, and slowly cinch down to spin in place, keeping tips slightly longer than butts. Make several turns ahead of butts, pack everything back tightly against tail using fingers or packing tool.

STEP 4 Spin chartreuse hair up remaining shank, packing bundles tightly against collar. Leave enough space behind eye for whip knot.

STEP 5 Carefully shave underside flat with razor blade, being careful not to cut thread.

STEP 6 Shape conical body ½ to ¾ inches at collar, tapering down to eye. The top can be rounded or flat; rounded head pushes more water. When trimming collar, leave all tips intact except on underside. Goop doll eyes onto either side. Apply floatant before using.

VARIATIONS

Bill's Redneck Slider can be tied in a number of great color combinations. Some of his favorites include orange, root beer, brown, and tan. Trussell likes to match the color of the body and tail, and add a contrasting collar. Marabou or saddle hackles can be substituted for the bucktail, wool for the deer-hair head.

B&R Diver

RAY CHAPPA & BILL SLOUGH

MATERIALS:

Hook:	Mustad 34007, No. 4
Thread:	Flymaster, orange
Tail:	Fuzzy marabou, orange
	Straight fibers from the tip of a marabou feather, black 2 grizzly saddle hackles, orange
	Flashabou, gold
Head:	Deer body hair, dark brown
	Deer body hair, orange
Floatant:	Watershed or equivalent

RAY CHAPA IS A FRIEND AND BONA FIDE FLY-FISHING NUT.
He captured the essence of fly-fishing the Texas coast when he said, "In the course of a fly-fisherman's life, sooner or later the numbers of fish become unimportant while the method used increases in value. Nine times out of 10, I will tie on this pattern when fishing a shallow flat. A U-shaped wake caused by a redfish's nose bulging up out of the water pursuing the fly is one of the most awesome sights on the coast. One topwater hookup equals 10 other hookups, in my opinion."

When developing this pattern, Chapa, an excellent fly-tier in his own right, sought out Bill Slough, known for his deft hand at crafting deer hair. Consequently, many folks think that B&R stands for "Bill and Ray," but actually the pattern is named for the Brown & Root Flats, a shallow-water haunt of many fly-fishers located between Port Aransas and Aransas Pass.

Chapa was quick to give credit to Larry Dahlberg, who developed the original pattern, the Dahlberg Diver. Chapa and Slough introduced several small changes that made it more conducive to Texas flats fishing. The size was scaled down to work well in calf-deep water. Most importantly, the color combination was fine-tuned after countless hours on the water. As testament to the pattern's effectiveness, Chapa pointed out that he was beaten in a one-fly tournament by a friend fishing a B&R Diver.

The fly is extremely durable and will hold up to the crushing jaws of a redfish. The collar forces the fly down into the water during the retrieve. At rest, it floats to the surface.

It is sometimes difficult to get a tailing red's attention with a sinking fly; a loud pop with this deer-hair pattern definitely gets their attention. The B&R Diver is also a great choice when "prospecting" sandy potholes in grass beds.

STEP 1

STEP 2

STEP 3

STEP 4

STEP 5

STEP 6

Once a redfish is pursuing the fly, do not change your stripping rate. It is important to maintain the pace until the fish has eaten the fly. Strip-strike the fish after you feel pressure on the line. Chapa urged that anglers not raise their rod to set the hook; many redfish have been lost by a premature strike. Due to their under-slung mouths, redfish often follow a surface fly and hit it repeatedly. Make sure you do not pull it out of the strike zone in your excitement.

TYING INSTRUCTIONS

STEP 1 Lay thread base 2/3 back from eye to bend. Tie shank-length orange marabou bundle atop thread base.

STEP 2 Tie equal length black marabou atop orange marabou.

STEP 3 Tie orange grizzly hackles slightly longer than marabou down either side, slight down slant.

STEP 4 Tie several strands gold Flashabou either side of hackles.

STEP 5 Spin 1 large or 2 small deer hair bundles in front of tail. Spin orange deer hair to eye, tie off.

STEP 6 Carefully shave underside flat with razor blade, being careful not to cut thread. Trim orange with scissors hair into symmetrical cone shape. Leave brown hair longer, trim into collar of even thickness.

VARIATIONS

You can tie the pattern in any contrasting colors you prefer. The orange and brown combination has proven the most effective for redfish.

Brooks' Caribou Slider

BROOKS BOULDIN

MATERIALS:

Hook:	Mustad 34011, No. 6
Thread:	Danville's flat waxed nylon, white
Weedguard:	Hard Mason, 16 pound
Tail:	Squirrel tail, gray Krystal Flash, pearl Grizzly hackles (number 3 grade)
Body:	Caribou hair

FLOATING SEA GRASS HAS PLAGUED COASTAL ANGLERS EVER since our ancestors first started casting for Jurassic trout. At no time is this more evident than during the summer season when, sea grasses are in full bloom.

"I have always enjoyed fishing deer-hair bugs in the summer, but I got tired of picking grass off of them after every cast," Brooks Bouldin said. "Surely, there had to be something better."

The Caribou Slider was the "something better" Bouldin came up with. "The pointed silhouette, combined with a double weedguard, makes this pattern virtually weedless." Bouldin said. "The knot used to connect the leader to the fly is the only thing that can possible snag any grass."

The slider can be tied with deer hair, but Bouldin chose caribou hair because it is more buoyant and easier to shape with a razor blade, and the color is a bit lighter.

The stiletto-shaped slider is designed for shin-deep water or less, where you do not need a loud pop to get a fish's attention. A heavy fly will often spook fish in such shallow water, but the Caribou Slider lands very softly.

Bouldin fishes the Caribou Slider differently depending on how shallow and spooky the fish are. Typically, he casts 1-2 feet in front of a fish and retrieves with irregular 2- to 3-inch strips. "Sometimes just a twitch is all that is needed for them to eat," he said.

STEP 1

STEP 2

STEP 3

STEP 4

STEP 5

TYING INSTRUCTIONS

STEP 1 Start thread as shown, tie 2 pieces Hard Mason on either side. Wrap thread halfway down bend. Tie squirrel tail atop thread wraps. Add 10-12 pieces Krystal Flash to tail, trim to length.

STEP 2 Tie 4 grizzly hackles, 2 on either side, splayed outward.

STEP 3 Beginning at tail, spin caribou hair forward. Pack hair tightly and repeat, leaving 1/16 inch space behind eye to tie off weedguard.

STEP 4 Carefully shave underside flat with razor blade, being careful not to cut thread. Tie down double weedguard behind eye.

STEP 5 Trim body into long, tapered, cone. Leave tips in ear long to blend with the tail.

VARIATIONS

Deer hair can be substituted for caribou hair.

Naiser Slider

REGGIE SHEFFIELD

MATERIALS:

Hook:	Mustad 34007 or TMC 811s, No. 4 or 6
Thread:	Danville Fly Master Plus, chartreuse
Eyes:	Lead dumb bell eyes, yellow with black pupil, 1/50 -5/32 ounce
Tail:	Grizzly hackles, chartreuse Grizzly hackles, white
Flash:	Holographic Fly Fiber Krystal Flash, chartreuse Krystal Flash, black
Wing/Body:	Deer hair, white Deer hair, chartreuse
Head	Deer hair, chartreuse

BEFORE A BONEFISH TRIP TO THE CHRISTMAS ISLANDS, Reggie Sheffield outfitted himself with an array of fly-tying equipment so he could crank out a bunch of Crazy Charlies. Once behind his new vise, he found he lacked patience and had way too many thumbs.

Time passed and a company acquisition left this financial officer unemployed with extra time on his hands. It was during this unintended sabbatical that Sheffield dug his vise out of storage and taught himself to spin and stack deer hair.

Good friend Captain Chuck Naiser had made the successful transition from businessman to fly-fishing guide at about that same time. Sheffield mailed Naiser some of his new deer-hair flies, and soon after Naiser inquired if Sheffield could craft something new for him.

High on Naiser's list of desirable characteristics was a fly that could be fished in heavy grass without fouling, and still be easy to cast. Clouser Minnows are sometimes hard for the fish to find in thick grass, and Naiser also wanted something with more "presence" in the water.

The fruit of Sheffield's efforts was the Naiser Slider. The little pattern became so popular that it launched Reggie Sheffield into the commercial tying business. Increasing demand eventually outstripped Sheffield's production capabilities and larger interests took over, allowing Sheffield to concentrate on tying custom flies.

"The Naiser Slider was designed for sight-casting," Sheffield said. "It is for fishing in a foot of water or less. The deer-hair head makes a quiet presentation without spooking the fish."

Sheffield likes to fish the pattern with short strips, typically 6-8 inches, but stressed he uses no set pattern. "I don't want the retrieve to be mechanical," he said. "I want the fly to dart around just like a small baitfish ."

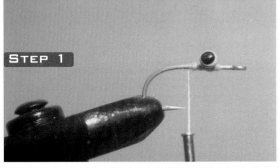

Sheffield's best success with the Naiser Sliders has been with chartreuse/white and pink/white colorations.

TYING INSTRUCTIONS

STEP 1 Figure-8 wrap eyes as shown.

STEP 2 Select 2 matching grizzly hackles and 2 matching white hackles of equal size. Tie one solid and one grizzly hackle on each side so feathers splay outward.

STEP 3 Fold 2 strands Holographic Fly Fiber around thread, tie on one side behind eyes. Repeat on other side. Repeat sequence using 3 strands chartreuse, 2 strands black flash. Nip ends of flash different lengths for tapered effect.

STEP 4 Cut white deer hair bundle, brush away underfur, even the tips. Hold bundle firmly in place, make two loose wraps, pull down snugly on thread so hair flares, keep tips longer than butts. (Note: You are stacking the hair, not spinning it, so do not let go of the bundle while pulling down on thread.)

STEP 5 Rotate vise. Repeat step on other using chartreuse hair. Rotate vise. Wind thread forward ahead of eyes. Tie off behind hook eye, head cement thread wraps.

STEP 6 Remove fly from vise. Trim head to shape with razor blade. Avoid cutting all long tips, which form part of tail.

VARIATIONS

Bead chain eyes can be substituted for lead dumbbell eyes. In addition to chartreuse and white, Sheffield ties the Naiser Slider in hot pink and white.

CHAPTER 9

Benthic Worms

Skippy's Lug Worm

CAPTAIN SKIPPER RAY

MATERIALS:

Hook:	Mustad 34007, No. 4 or 6
Thread:	6/0, olive or black
Body:	Krystal Flash, olive or motor oil
	Grizzly hackle, yellow
Glue:	5-minute epoxy

SEVERAL HOURS OF CASTING TO CRUISING REDFISH LEFT
Captain Skipper Ray pitching a shutout one afternoon. "The sun was right, the wind was right, everything was perfect, except the fish wouldn't bite," he recalled. "I tried 10-12 patterns that day, but got the cold shoulder on everything I threw. I finally caught a fish on a chartreuse and white Clouser Minnow and when I bent down to unhook it, I found worms sticking out of the fish's throat. Using my forceps, I retrieved a few to study.

"I kept that fish, and when I cleaned it, it was full of the worms." The partially digested worms in the stomach formed an olive-green "gall." "Having seen that gall inside countless redfish, I figured I was onto something."

Ray consulted with Captain Eric Glass, a good friend and former biology teacher, about the worms. Glass pronounced the worms *Arenicola cristata,* or in layman's terms, "lug worm."

Arenicola cristata is a polychaete worm that burrows in the sand and feeds on bottom sediments. Neither Ray nor Glass could confirm if redfish smell the worms' vent stack or senses the current from its burrow. They just know they eat a lot of the worms. Ray suggested looking for the worms' vent stacks in hard sandy areas.

"The fish raced to my new pattern as if they hadn't eaten for days, only to bolt away when they got close," he said. After a dozen similar refusals, the light bulb went off. "Lug worms don't swim!"

"The secret to fishing Skippy's Lug Worm is to strip the fly only until you get the fish's attention, then stop all movement until the fish eats," Ray said.

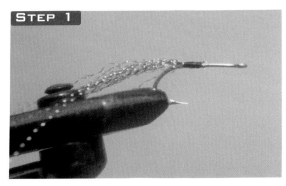

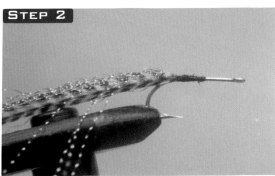

TYING INSTRUCTIONS

STEP 1 Start thread above hook point. Tie twenty 2-inch strands Krystal Flash.

STEP 2 Tie ¼-inch wide yellow grizzly hackle as shown.

STEP 3 Tie another small bundle Krystal Flash in at bend. Wrap thread forward to eye. Wrap Krystal Flash to eye, tie off and trim.

STEP 4 Epoxy shank, rotate until tacky. Palmer hackle forward to eye, ⅛-inch separation between turns, embedding stem in epoxy. Tie off at eye, whip finish. Trim tail to length as needed. Overall fly should be 2¼ to 2½ inches.

CHAPTER 10
Jetty & Surf Patterns

Zaftig Shrimp

CHARLES LEVINSON

MATERIALS:

Hook:	Mustad 92611, No. 1/0 or larger (extra long shank)
Thread:	Flymaster, pink & white
Weight:	Lead wire, .002 inch diameter
Antennae:	Brown kip Flashabou, gold Javelina hide bristles
Eyes:	4mm black beads mounted on either end of 20-pound Hard Mason, 1 inch long
Body:	Aunt Lydia's yarn, creme color – 28 inch length Medium Ice Chenille – 18 inch length
Carapace:	Mylar tubing (.025 .03 inch diameter), pink – 2.5 inches long

CHARLES LEVINSON WASN'T BORN WITH A ROD AND REEL IN his hand, but he got one as soon as he could. Having fished the Rockport area with his dad since the late 1940s, he has built up a sizable knowledge base about fishing the middle Texas coast, both bay and surf. A relatively recent convert to fly-fishing with a mere ten years tenure, Levinson is now putting his knowledge to good use creating innovative saltwater patterns.

"The first time you see this fly, you are going to start looking for a frying pan," Levinson quipped. "I have been fooling around with a shrimp pattern up for use in the surf. Wait 'til you see this....

The Zaftig (pronounced "zof-tig") Shrimp gets its name from a Yid-dish word meaning "well endowed." Depending on hook size, the pattern can be scaled up to 6 inches long.

Levinson fished other shrimp patterns in the past, and found they often ran on their sides or even upside-down. He sought to find a shrimp pattern that would run true. The problem was that the other patterns did not have a way to stabilize themselves. Levinson solved this problem with a pair of large eye stems.

While tinkering with this pattern, Levinson would stop at a bait stand on his way home from a fishing trip and buy a single large shrimp to study. "I tried to figure out how to tie something that would imitate a shrimp's movement," he said.

"A north wind knocks the surf down and allows you to cast just about any direction, but during the summer when south or southeast winds blow, I try to stand on a sand bar and cast parallel to it into a gut. Redfish sometimes shadow pods of mullet in the surf. If there are fish in the gut, they'll hammer this pattern."

Levinson prefers fishing the Zaftig Shrimp with a sink tip or intermediate line in the surf. A short 4- to 5-foot leader

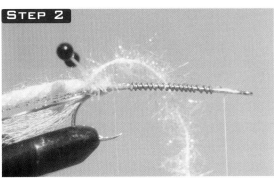

is all that is necessary.

"If you are going to throw a large version of the fly, I wouldn't use anything lighter than a 9-weight," he said. "The fly is heavy and you need a larger rod to cast it. I've caught some really big redfish on this fly, and they really beat me up."

Levinson recommended fishing the Zaftig Shrimp with a slow 4- to 5-inch strip-and-pause retrieve when the surf is smooth. In rough conditions, he suggested a much faster retrieve.

TYING INSTRUCTIONS

STEP 1 Bend shank slightly toward point. Start pink thread as shown, wind forward ⅛ inch. Lay lead wire on thread base, secure end with more thread wraps. Make 12 wire wraps in loose spiral, cement in place. Wrap thread forward to bend. Tie kip on bend at down angle. Add Flashabou atop kip. Tie in javelina bristles on either side, extending 1 hook length. Wrap eye assembly above hook point.

STEP 2 Tie Ice Chenille between eyes and tail, followed by yarn. Head cement eye and antennae assembly. Mount white thread at hook eye, move pink thread out of way.

STEP 3 Wrap yarn bend-to-eye in to build up body, thick at head, tapering to eye. Tie off, do not clip thread. Wrap chenille head-to-eye, tie off. Trim white thread.

STEP 4 Flatten Mylar tubing atop shrimp body, secure both ends with pink thread. Unravel rear tubing end. Segment body with windings spaced ³⁄₁₆" apart. Tie off, head cement entire Mylar surface.

VARIATIONS

The Zaftig Shrimp is just as at home on a No. 6 hook as on a 2/0. Tie the pattern on small hooks for sight-casting in the bays, and on large hooks for fishing the surf and jetties. Mustad 92611 hooks have a slight offset which can be straightened in a vise if you prefer. Levinson suggested tying the pattern in white, pink, and brown to match the different types of shrimp.

Spanish Macarena

RAY CHAPA

MATERIALS:

Hook:	Mustad 34007, No. 2
Thread:	3/0, chartreuse
Eye:	7/32 lead, red with black pupil
Wing:	Fly Fur, white
Middle wing:	Flashabou, Ocean Green # 6922
Lip:	20-pound mono Softex

FELLOW SCRIBE RAY CHAPA IS A WELL-KNOWN FLY-FISHING guru who lives in San Antonio. This former President of the Alamo Fly Fishers learned by doing with good friends and mentors in the club.

Their mantra was, "No water is too far, too shallow, or too hot." It was this attitude that enabled them to develop successful techniques for fly-fishing the jetties. Chapa and his fellow jetty rats make the three-hour dash to Port Aransas whenever the tides and wind are right.

Lacking a pattern specifically designed for fishing the rocks, Chapa developed the Spanish Macarena. A Clouser Minnow derivation, the fly is heavily weighted and dressed with Fly Fur. "White Fly Fur has more action than bucktail, and is more translucent in the water." Chapa said. "And the bill causes the fly to swim erratically. "Unlike most Clouser flies, which are tied fairly sparsely, the Spanish Macarena is fully dressed. That makes it push more water and attract more attention."

The full coat of Fly Fur provides another benefit: durability. Members of the toothy mackerel family shred most flies like Weedeaters run amok. Chapa noted that each Spanish Mackerel and kingfish caught reduced the amount of Fly Fur left attached to the hook. Because it is tied generously, it can handle multiple fish before being retired.

Although the Spanish Macarena is large and heavily weighted, Chapa said an 8-weight rod will cast it with ease due to the height advantage the jetties provide. Somewhat in jest, he noted that hooking yourself or someone else is as likely as hooking a fish when jetties are crowded. The need for caution goes without saying.

Chapa suggested experimenting with the retrieve until you find something the fish like. He said that mackerel typically prefer a fast retrieve. Depending on water depth and current, Chapa lets the fly to sink to a count 10, 20, or even 30 before beginning the retrieve.

Since many jetty predators have sharp teeth, Chapa suggested fishing the fly behind a 20-pound-test mini-

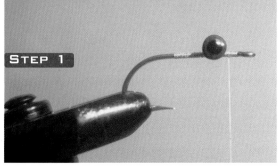

STEP 1

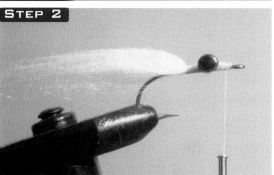

STEP 2

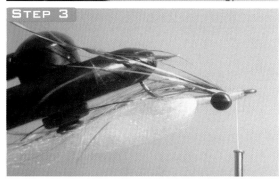

STEP 3

STEP 4

STEP 5

STEP 6

mum bite tippet. He upgrades to 60- or 80-pound monofilament when he starts losing flies to bite-offs.

To date, Chapa and friends have caught over a dozen different species on the Spanish Macarena, including a tarpon and one false albacore that became a Texas state record in 1998.

TYING INSTRUCTIONS

STEP 1 Flatten barb and sharpen hook. Build two thread bumps to seat eyes. FIgure-8 wrap eyes as shown. Zap-a-Gap eye wraps.

STEP 2 Tie in substantial amount Fly Fur for lower wing.

STEP 3 Rotate vise, hook point up. Tie in generous Flashabou portion.

STEP 4 Tie upper wing as shown, again using a substantial material, trim.

STEP 5 Tie 4-inch mono between the hook eye and lead eyes. Fashion U-shaped mono lip in so it extends below shank as shown. Imperfectly aligned loop is desired. Trim excess mono.

STEP 6 Fill mono loop with Softex, dry 15 minutes. Add two more coats to complete.

VARIATIONS

In the event of short strikes, Chapa suggested trimming the length of the wing to just beyond the hook.

113

Patterns

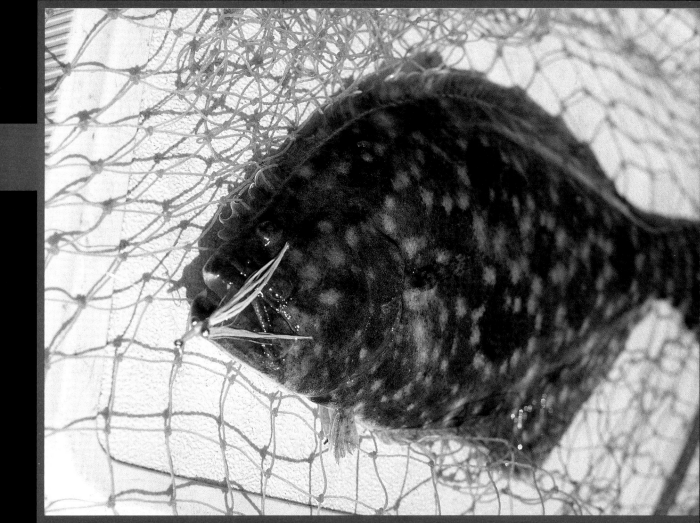

Flounder Candy

JIM GREEN

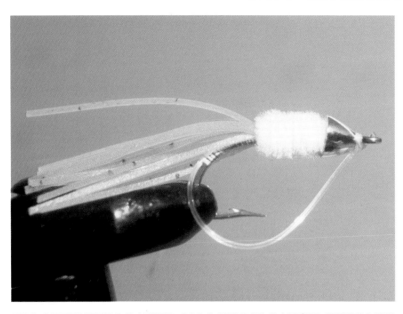

MATERIALS:

Hook:	Mustad 34007, No. 2
Thread:	6/0 Uni, white
Cone:	Silver or gold, large
Weedguard:	30-lb. Hard Mason monofilament
Tail:	Sili Legs, lime/black flake
Body:	Chenille, white

JIM GREEN WAS RAISED ON A HORSE RANCH. WHEN HE started tying flies in 1959, he got most of his tying materials from the animals on the ranch. The only source of information back then was the Herter's Catalog. Green fondly recalled there were three different vises available from the mail-order company. "One was $1.50, another was $3.50, and the third was $7.50," he said. "I couldn't come up with enough money for any of them, so I improvised with a curved pair of needlenose pliers held in place by a carpenter's vise."

Green is certainly an inventive type behind the vise. A retired biologist who was responsible for New Mexico, Arizona, and West Texas when he worked for the U. S. Fish and Wildlife Service, he now puts his scientific knowledge to good use crafting unique saltwater patterns.

"I developed the Flounder Candy specifically for fishing the mud flats on the backside of Rollover Pass," he said. "Since flounder lack a swim bladder, they cannot suspend in the water like other fish. Instead, they lie on the bottom and ambush shrimp and baitfish that come too close. They won't move very far to capture a meal, so I wanted a pattern that would stay down on the bottom. You can fish this pattern in water up to 10 feet deep."

Retrieving the Flounder Candy is a simple affair. Green likes to drag the pattern slowly over the bottom, or hop it so it kicks up little puffs of mud. He cautioned against fishing it in areas with oysters to avoid snagging on on the shell.

"When the tide changes over a muddy bottom, the water clarity suffers quickly," he said. "It is important to have a pattern that the fish can sense or feel when they can not see that far."

In addition to flounder, Green has used the pattern successfully on speckled trout around the wells in Trinity Bay.

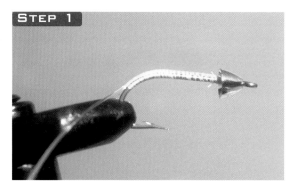

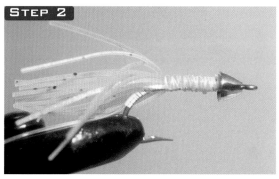

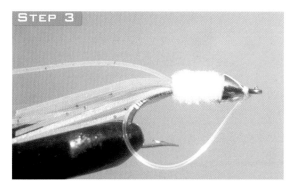

TYING INSTRUCTIONS

STEP 1 Slide cone onto hook. Tie mono weedguard on shank as shown, wrapping down bend.

STEP 2 Tie thick Sili Legs bundle for tail, extending 1 hook-length beyond bend. Tie chenille atop Sili Legs above hook point. (Not pictured.)

STEP 3 Wrap chenille forward to cone, tie off. Tie off weedguard between eye and cone.

VARIATIONS

The Flounder Candy can be tied in a variety of contrasting color schemes. The most productive include a white or fluorescent body with a florescent pink or strawberry red tail. A spinnerbait skirt can be substituted for Sili Legs.

117

Offshore
Patterns

Jim's Bluewater Squid

JIM GREEN

MATERIALS:

Hook:	Mustad 34007, No. 2/0 – 4/0
Thread:	Uni Big Fly, white
Tail:	Medium mylar cord (unravelled), pearl
	Sili Legs, sand orange/black flake
Eyes:	Umpqua presentation eyes, pearl or Wapsi dumbbell eyes, pearl
Body:	Medium or large chenille, florescent white
	Tinsel chenille, pearl

AS OFTEN AS HE CAN, JIM GREEN JOURNEYS FROM HIS home in Tyler to the coast. Like many before him, the call of the deep entices him beyond the jetties to explore the vast expanses of the Gulf.

Jim's Bluewater Squid was designed for the pelagic species that roam offshore.

"I primarily use this pattern when fishing around the rigs," Green said. "Once I get to the rig, I like to chum a while to draw the fish in close to the boat. Because this fly is heavy, I want to minimize the casting distance. This pattern wasn't meant to be cast with an 8-weight rod."

Green suggested using long, straight strips to fish Jim's Bluewater Squid, pausing just a bit between strips to give it a jigging action. Depending on the fish, he sometimes tucks his rod under one arm and uses a fast two-hand retrieve.

As of this writing, Green and friends have used the pattern to fooled Spanish mackerel, blacktip shark, barracuda, and dorado. He has also hooked several large fish that couldn't be turned with a 12-weight rod. "I am sure it was a 150-pound wahoo," he said with a wink. "If you are going to tell a whopper, it might as well be a big one."

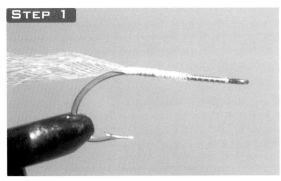

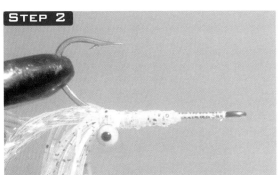

TYING INSTRUCTIONS

STEP 1 Tie medium mylar tubing as shown, unravel end.

STEP 2 (Vise in photo rotated only to show detail.) Tie Sili Legs atop mylar tubing, leave full length. Tie eyes ahead of Sili Legs.

STEP 3 Tie white chenille 2/3 down shank. Wrap chenille to eyes, then back to starting point, forming carrot-shaped body. Tie Tinsel chenille, wind to hook eye, tie off.

Killer B

BRIAN HANDLIN

MATERIALS:

Hook:	Gamakatsu SL11 3H, No. 3/0 to 5/0
Thread:	Danville, white flat waxed nylon
Tail:	Saddle hackles white Flashabou, pearl or silver Bucktail, white
Eyes:	Painted lead dumb-bell
Body:	Deer hair, white

WHILE MANAGING AN OUTFITTERS STORE IN THE FLORIDA Keys, Brian Handlin had the occasion to meet television personality Mark Sosin. A year prior, Handlin had developed a bucktail pattern that Sosin caught many Spanish mackerel on.

Sosin was bringing his crew back to Florida to film another segment of "Saltwater Journal," but this time the quarry was sharks. Handlin developed the Killer-B specifically for the show, and the host declared it a successful pattern. To date, Sosin has featured the Killer-B in two different segments of "Saltwater Journal."

The Killer-B possesses a deer hair head and lead eyes that make it suspend in the strike zone. Handlin suggested using a multi-strand wire leader between leader and fly to prevent shark-tooth cut-offs.

Handlin prefers to draw in sharks by chumming. Chunks of barracuda are his favorite shark chum. "For whatever reason, sharks from miles around are drawn in by the smell," Handlin said. He also uses chunks of jackfish, which are very oily.

"If I am using barracuda for chum, I use a solid white Killer-B, but if I am chumming with jackfish, I switch to an orange pattern with gold Flashabou. When a shark sees the pattern, you don't have to move it much. If the shark circles, try waiting until it can see the fly then strip it away quickly. This typically will provoke a strike."

In addition to sharks, Handlin has used the Killer-B to catch tarpon and dorado.

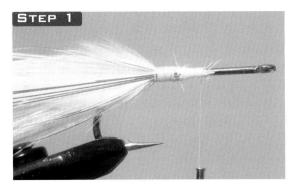

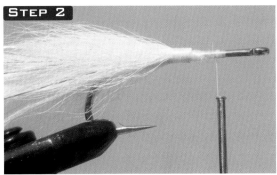

TYING INSTRUCTIONS

STEP 1 Start thread ½ inch ahead of hook point, wrap back to bend. Tie 3-5 saddle hackles on either side, splaying outward. Add 4-6 strands Flashabou on either side.

STEP 2 Tie bucktail collar around hackles, extending half length of hackles.

STEP 3 Beginning at tail, spin hair on shank. Add 2-3 bundles, packing each down tightly, stopping ½ inch from eye. Figure-8 wrap as shown, leaving space behind hook eye. Zap-A-Gap eye wraps.

STEP 4 Spin hair behind eyes, flaring around them. Do not spin hair ahead of eyes. Whip finish ahead of eyes, add Zap-A-Gap.

STEP 5 Trim head to shape with razor blade.

VARIATIONS

A Mustad 34007 (No. 4/0) can be substituted for the Gamakatsu hook.

CHAPTER 13
Spoon Flies

Epoxy Moron

CAPTAIN SCOTT GRAHAM

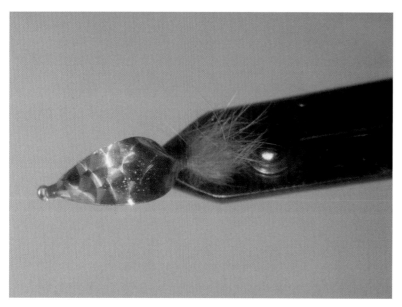

MATERIALS:

Hook:	Mustad 34011, No. 4
Thread:	Flat waxed nylon, color to match tail
Rib:	Flat braided nylon tubing, color to match body
Tail:	Rabbit fur, pink or chartreuse
Underbody:	Holographic or prismatic tape, gold
Overbody:	5-minute epoxy

CAPTAIN SCOTT GRAHAM MAY BE THE ONLY GUIDE IN THE state who charters fly-fishing trips in freshwater, cold water, and saltwater. Graham seems to have put his quarter-century of fly-fishing experience to good use, holding the state record for rainbow trout as well as two previous state fly rod records that have since been broken.

"I grew up throwing spoons with conventional tackle," Graham said. "When I started fly-fishing on the Texas coast, I used a Kirk's Wobbler from Orvis. The Dupree Spoon Fly hadn't hit the shelves in Texas yet, and when I came across some prismatic tape at an auto parts store, a light bulb went off."

Regardless of who was first to develop this style of fly, the Epoxy Moron seems to be a hit with the fish. "It is my confidence fly." Graham said. "I catch fish on this pattern when nothing else works."

Graham remembered fishing a prototype of the Epoxy Moron on a trip with Jim Dailey, an avid fly-fisherman and retired fisheries biologist who spent over 30 years working for the Texas Parks and Wildlife Department. "The first day, after I caught a boatload of fish, Dailey started grousing about letting him use one of the new flies. "So, I let him borrow the fly I was using the next day. Together, we caught and released nearly 75 redfish in two days on that one fly."

Although the name of the fly is the Epoxy Moron, many of his clients refer to the pattern as the Scott Spoon.

Graham offered several helpful hints about fishing the flashy pattern. "First, a loop knot allows the fly to wobble back and forth through the water," he said. "Cinch knots really limit the action of the fly."

Because the shank is bent, the fly rises when retrieved. The correct hook shape is essential. If the completed fly spins in the water, bend the hook more.

Graham suggested stripping the fly then pausing to allow it to flutter toward the bottom. "The fish often nail it on the fall," he said. "I have even had reds eat it wile it was sitting motionless on the bottom. Vary your retrieve until you find something the fish like."

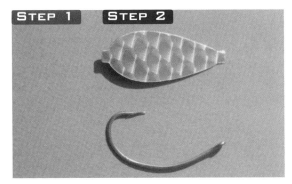

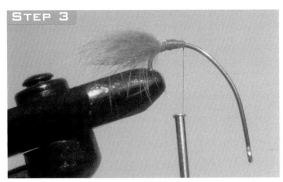

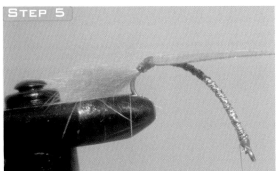

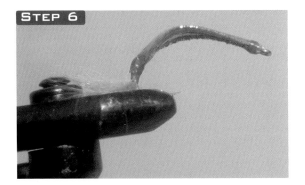

TYING INSTRUCTIONS

STEP 1 Bend hook to shape.

STEP 2 Cut out small prismatic tape section, bend in half and press sticky sides together. Lay bent hook on tape for guide to trace spoon-shaped pattern. Cut out pattern with scissors, leaving ⅛-inch tabs on either end.

STEP 3 Tie rabbit fur tail at bend.

STEP 4 Tie flat braid and rear tape pattern tab, tie off.

STEP 5 Restart thread near eye. Wrap flat braid to eye, add a half hitch, tie down front tab, whip finish.

STEP 6 Epoxy body with thin coat, being careful of tail. Rotate until dry.

VARIATIONS

Different colored rabbit fur and prismatic tape can be substituted.

Scott's Special

CAPTAIN SCOTT SOMMERLATTE

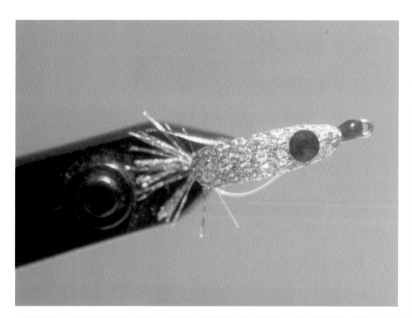

MATERIALS:

Hook:	Mustad 34011, No. 4
Thread:	Flymaster Plus, red
Weedguard:	12-lb. Hard Mason
Body:	Wapsi Flexicord holographic tubing (1/4 inch), gold
Glue:	Devcon 2 Ton epoxy, clear (15 minute working time)
Eyes:	Prismatic stick-on eyes (1/4 inch), red

AFTER SERVING HIS COUNTRY IN THE UNITED STATES Coast Guard, Captain Scott Sommerlatte found another career on the water: guiding coastal fly-fishermen and duck hunters. An accomplished wildlife photographer, this bright young guide has an eye for detail. He brings that focus to the tying bench as evidenced by the a number of productive saltwater patterns for the Texas coast. One of his go-to patterns is the Scott's Special.

"I always liked the idea of a spoon fly, but found that all of the patterns available in stores either twisted the line badly, were too wind resistant, weighed too much, and weren't very weedless," Sommerlatte said.

Two years of tinkering went into the development of the Scott's Special. "I felt that the pattern needed a narrower profile," he said. "This helped reduce the fly's weight, which made for much quieter presentation."

The bend in the hook serves several important functions. First, it helps keep the fly from spinning. Second, causes the hook to lodge in the corner of a redfish's mouth. "I am especially proud that I have never gill-hooked a redfish with this pattern," Sommerlatte said.

A loop knot, such as the Mono-Loop Knot, should be used when fishing the Scott's Special to ensure optimum action.

When sight-casting to a cruising or tailing red, Sommerlatte lets the fly sink to the fish's depth before stripping. He bases the retrieve on the fish's reaction. One successful technique is a series of short 2-inch strips. Another is using 4- to 18-inch strips. It is important to pause between strips to allow the fly to flutter back toward bottom. Most strikes come on the fall.

Sommerlatte recommended this pattern for beginning fly-fisherman that may not have well-developed casting skills. "Redfish love this pattern and will eat it even if the cast is a little off," he said.

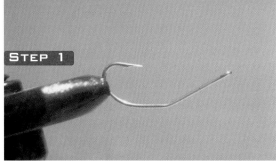

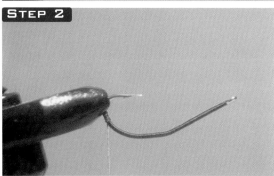

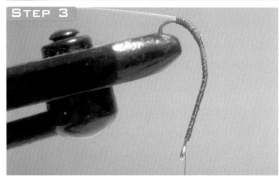

TYING INSTRUCTIONS

STEP 1 Bend hook to shape shown.

STEP 2 Lay down eye-to-bend thread base as shown. (Vise in photo rotated only to show detail.)

STEP 3 Tie in weedguard at bend. (Vise in photo readjusted to show detail.)

STEP 4 Lay Flexicord on shank, tie bend-to-eye. Tie off and trim. Leave ½ inch of Flexicord extending behind bend. Tie down front section of braid near eye, trim loose ends. Unravel braid and trim to length for tail.

STEP 5 Bring weedguard through eye, fold back along shank, secure with thread wraps. Trim weedguard and form tapered head, covering any exposed weedguared near eye. Add stick-on eye, holding in place with a clothespin.

STEP 6 Epoxy all surfaces, rotate until dry.

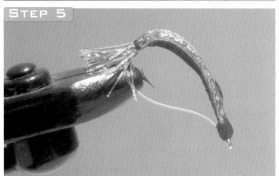

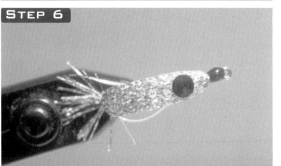

Texas State Records

SPECIES	WEIGHT (LBS.)	LENGTH (IN)	DATE
BARRACUDA, GREAT	16.69	46.50	9/15/98
BUMPER, ATLANTIC	0.16	7.90	7/11/00
CHUB, BERMUDA	3.63	18.13	9/6/01
COBIA	36.33	50.20	9/17/01
CROAKER, ATLANTIC	0.23	8.70	8/10/99
CUTLASSFISH, ATLANTIC	0.88	33.75	12/2/99
DOLPHIN	11.56	39.50	8/29/00
DRUM, BLACK	7.50	26.00	10/4/01
DRUM, RED	28.10	41.00	2/15/01
FLOUNDER, SOUTHERN	5.00	24.00	11/26/99
JACK, ALMACO	.40	9.75	7/1/00
JACK, CREVALLE	19.38	37.00	12/11/99
JACK, HORSE-EYE	8.70	29.13	6/17/01
KINGFISH, GULF	0.63	13.50	6/16/99
KINGFISH, SOUTHERN	1.19	14.25	7/9/00
LADYFISH	2.20	22.25	5/28/01
MACKEREL, KING	19.94	45.00	8/29/00
MACKEREL, SPANISH	4.90	30.00	9/16/00
PERCH, SILVER	0.25	8.25	7/14/00
PINFISH	0.35	8.50	8/17/00
POMPANO, FLORIDA	3.91	21.00	7/3/00
RUNNER, RAINBOW	.54	12.63	8/17/01
SARDINE, SCALED	0.10	6.50	8/20/99
SEATROUT, SAND	0.75	12.88	7/8/00
SEATROUT, SPOTTED	10.20	33.75	5/29/01
SHARK, SILKY	8.60	34.00	8/21/99
SHEEPSHEAD	5.27	20.50	9/2/00
SNAPPER, RED	4.30	19.25	8/21/99
SNOOK	5.56	27.50	3/28/99
SPADEFISH, ATLANTIC	2.07	14.75	7/21/00
TUNA, BLACKFIN	19.10	33.25	11/8/01
TUNNY, LITTLE	5.14	25.00	11/7/99

Caught on a Fly Rod

WATER BODY	ANGLER	FLY
Gulf of Mexico	Whitner Dieterich	Streamer
Gulf of Mexico	Kenneth Thyssen	Hare's Ear Nymph
Gulf of Mexico	Jim Darnell	Unknown
Gulf of Mexico	Robert Sloan	Unknown
Lower Laguna Madre	Charles Miller	Clouser Minnow
Laguna Madre	Thomas Sheehan	Chartruese/white Clouser Deep Minnow
Gulf of Mexico	Jeffery Pierce	Unknown
Lower Laguna Madre	William Williams	Unknown
Lower Laguna Madre	Scott Graham	Unknown
Galveston Bay	Jon Parks	Clouser Minnow
Gulf of Mexico	Steve Welborn	Unknown
Gulf of Mexico	Lindsay Sharpe	Chartruese/white Clouser Minnow
Gulf of Mexico	Robert Sloan	Unknown
Gulf of Mexico	Jon Parks	Clouser Deep Minnow
Galveston Bay	Kenneth Thyssen	Unknown
Lower Laguna Madre	Skipper Ray	Unknown
Gulf of Mexico	Jeffery Pierce	Unknown
Gulf of Mexico	Phil Shook	Deceiver
Gulf of Mexico	Kenneth Thyssen	Glass minnow
Gulf of Mexico	Kenneth Thyssen	Unknown
Gulf of Mexico	Gary Shelton Jr.	Pink rattling Clouser Minnow
Gulf of Mexico	Kenneth Thyssen	Unknown
Corpus Christi	John Jackman	Chartreuse/white Clouser Minnow
Gulf of Mexico	Kenneth Thyssen	Unknown
Lower Laguna Madre	Carl Rowland	Unknown
Gulf of Mexico	Robert Sloan	Streamer
Gulf of Mexico	Gary Shelton Jr.	Clouser Minnow
Gulf of Mexico	Robert Sloan	Streamer
Lower Laguna Madre	Larry Haines	Haines Pilchard
Gulf of Mexico	Connie Mack Moran	Chartreuse Clouser Minnow
Gulf of Mexico	Barry Box	Unknown
Gulf of Mexico	Robert Sloan	Tube Dart

Fly-fishing Clubs

MOST OF THE FLY-FISHING CLUBS IN THE STATE OF TEXAS ARE affiliated with the Federation of Fly Fishers (FFF). FFF is a non-profit organization that promotes several core values, including conservation of all fish in all waters, commitment to solving fisheries problems at the grass-roots level, and that fly-fishing is the most fun way to fish. Additional information about FFF can be found on their web site, www.fedfly-fisher.org. With the exception of the Golden Spread Fly Fishers in Amarillo, the clubs in Texas are part of the FFF Southern Council. Up-to-date information can be found on their web site, www.southerncouncilfff.org.

These clubs offer a wealth of knowledge to the novice angler. Clubs generally have fresh- and saltwater outings where members can enjoy time on the water together. You will find that most club members are very active fly-tiers. Who better to learn from than a seasoned veteran? If you are new to fly-fishing or just new to your area, check out one of the local clubs. They will be glad to help you get started.

Statewide: Texas Women Fly Fishers
Constance Whiston, President
cwhiston@mail.io.com
Meetings rotate in six different Texas cities.

Austin: Austin Fly Fishers
Alan Bray, President
brayfisher@aol.com
Web site: www.austinflyfishers.com

Amarillo: Golden Spread Fly Fishers
http://home.amaonline.com/gsff

Bryan: Brazos Valley Fly Fishers
http://www.mmrgenetics.com/bvff/

Corpus Christi: Coastal Bend Fly Fishers
Paul Swacina, President
pswacina@brinandbrin.com

Dallas: Dallas Fly Fishers
Web sites: http://www.dallas-flyfishers.org/

Fort Worth: Fort Worth Fly Fishers
Johnny Walker, President
web site: www.iflyfish.com/fwff/

Houston: Texas Fly Fishers
Mike Eberhard, President

Kerrville: Hill County Fly Fishers
Clay Corder – President

Longview: East Texas Fly Fishers
Meetings: 2nd Tuesday, 6:30 PM,
Johnny Caces Seafood & Steak House,1501 E. Marshall Ave.
Lufkin

Pineywoods: Fly Fishers
Web site: http://freepages.outdoors.rootsweb.com/~wem1

San Antonio: Alamo Fly Fishers
Web site: http://www.thefishernet.com/affweb.htm

San Marcos: Central Texas Fly Fishers
Web site: www.ctff.org

Spring: Montgomery County Flyrodders
President: Dan Houchin, houc@chevron.com

Texarkana: Texarkana Area Fly Fishers
Meetings: 2nd Tuesday, 7PM, 319 Baylor (TDS Building)

Tyler: Tyler Fly Fishers (club in the process of reorganizing)
Larry Knackstedt, President
larry@domehomes.com

Victoria: Gulf Coast Flyrodders
Web site: http://www.viptx.net/flyrodders/

Waco: The Jack Sparks Central Texas Flyrodders
Web site: http//home.att.net/~m.b.brown/

Recommended Resources

Fly-fishing and fly-tying are lifetime pursuits because the learning never stops. A number of great books and videos are available that I would recommend to any angler, beginner to salty veteran. Keep in mind that some of these texts and videos cover exotic fish and destinations and at first glance may not appear to be germane to Texas, but they include pertinent information on tides, presentation, and technique--useful information for any saltwater fly-fisherman, whether they fish in Christmas Bay or the Christmas Islands.

BOOKS

Fly Fishing the Texas Coast: Backcountry Flats to Blue Water
Phil H. Shook, Chuck Scates, David Sams
ISBN 0-87108888-6
Pruett Publishing Co.

The Art of Fly Tying
John Van Vlient
ISBN 0-86573-043-1
Creative Publishing International

Prey
Designing & Tying New Imitations of Fresh & Saltwater Forage Fish
Carl Richards
ISBN 1-55821-332-5
Lyons & Burford, Publishers

101 Fly-Fishing Tips
Lefty Kreh
ISBN 1-58574-035-7
The Lyons Press

Flyfishing for Redfish
Captain John A. Kumiski
ISBN 0-9635118-2-3
Argonaut Publishing Company

Fly Fishing in Salt Water
Lefty Kreh
Rod Walinchus (Illustrator)
ISBN 1-55821-590-5
The Lyons Press

Saltwater Fly Tying
Frank Wentink
ISBN 1-55821-355-4
The Lyons Press

Longer Fly Casting
Lefty Kreh
Rod Walinchus (Illustrator)
ISBN 1-55821-127-6
The Lyons Press

Practical Saltwater Fly Fishing
Mark Sosin
ISBN 1-55821-043-1
Lyons & Burford, Publishers

Getting Hooked on the Flats, Texas Style
Roy L. Williams
Self Published

Saltwater Fly Patterns
Lefty Kreh
ISBN 1-55821-336-8
Lyons & Burford, Publishers

Presenting The Fly
Lefty Kreh
ISBN 1-55821-788-6
The Lyons Press

Bonefishing
Randall Kaufmann
ISBN 1-885212-13-5
Western Fisherman's Press

Fly Fishing the Tidewaters
Tom Earnhardt
ISBN 1-55821-393-7
Lyons & Buford, Publishers

Practical Fishing Knots II
Mark Sosin & Lefty Kreh
ISBN 1-55821-102-0
Lyons Press

VIDEOS

Fly Fishing for Redfish on the Texas Gulf Coast
Ray Box

Tying Techniques of Bob Clouser & Lefty Kreh
Volumes 1 & 2
Bob Clouser & Lefty Kreh

The Art of Fly Casting
Chico Fernandez

The Essence of Fly Casting
Volumes 1 & 2
Mel Krieger

Tying Saltwater Flies with Jimmy Nix
Jack Dennis
Volume 1 & 2

All New Fly Casting Technique
Lefty Kreh
Outdoor Safaris International Video

Acknowledgements

WRITING A BOOK IS A VERY TIME CONSUMING PROCESS. I learned firsthand that turning a manuscript into a finished text is an involved, and often tedious task. Writing your first book presents challenges over and above those faced by published authors. *Texas Saltwater Classics* would have never happened without the help and support from a lot of people.

I owe a huge debt of gratitude to Roy Neves who believed in me enough to publish *Texas Saltwater Classics*. He invested a significant amount of time researching the market, and then set out to produce the highest quality book that he could. I will forever be grateful for his faith in me as writer.

I would also like to thank Don Zaidle for his keen wordsmithing skills and high standards. Don edits my fly-fishing columns in *Texas Fish & Game* magazine, and is exacting in the use of the English language. He did a great job sharpening up the prose in *Texas Saltwater Classics*, and I am very appreciative of his hard work and mentoring style.

Words alone do not make for an interesting fly-tying book. Wendy Kipfmiller designed the layout for the text and made it pleasing to the eye. She was tremendous to work with, taking my abstract ideas and creating just the right look and feel. I appreciate very much her hard work and long hours behind the computer. I also appreciate the work of Doug Berry, Anna Campbell, and Amanda McCracken of *Texas Fish & Game*, who did the nuts and bolts placement of text and photos into the book.

I would be remiss if I did not thank the talented group of fly-tiers featured in this book. *Texas Saltwater Classics* would not be a reality without them. I appreciate everyone's upbeat attitude, no matter how many times I called to clarify details.

Several years ago, I joined the Texas Outdoor Writers Association and was immediately embraced by the best outdoors writers in the business. I expected to be treated like a newcomer, but instead was welcomed like one of the family. I would like to recognize the following communicators, both regional and national, for their coaching, encouragement, wisdom, and suggestions: Crispin Battles, Larry Bozka, Jonette Childs, Jim Darnell, Joe Doggett, Susan Ebert, Sugar Ferris, Bob Flood, Jim Foster, T. J. Greaney, Bink Grimes, Kendal Hemphill, Larry Hodge, Mike Holmes,

John Jefferson, Peter Jenkins, Leslie Kelly, Ben Kocian, Larry LeBlanc, Lee Leschper, Steve Lightfoot, Bob Lusk, Mark McDonald, Bill E. Mills, Chester Moore, Earl Nottingham, Bill Olson, Doug Pike, Judy Rider, Phil Shook, David Sikes, Thorne Sparkman, Ron Henry Strait, Shannon Tompkins, Reavis Wortham.

In addition, I would like to thank the following people for their friendship and help: Ted Baker, Mike Barbee, Dan Buckle, Betty Butler, Ray Box, Ken Brumbaugh, Ed Carman, Jim Dailey, Lon Deckard, Jack Denny, Marcos Enrique, Dale Fridy, O. C. Garza, Rueben Garza Jr., Phil Genova, Bruce Gillan, Anthony Grice, Tom Hargrave, Dave Hayward, Derek Howell, Charlie Jones, Jinger Knight, Eric Kraimer, Gib Little, Tom Lyons, Cary Marcus, Mark Marmon, Rosario Martinez, John Mazurkiewicz, Heather McAllister, Tom McDonnell, Darryl Menard, Joe Mendez, Sally Moffett, Kenny Murph, Chuck Naiser, Terry Neal, Mark Nichols, Patrick Nicosia Jr., Othell Owensby, Andy Packmore, Lance Robinson, Billy Sandifer, Jeff Shatto, Kevin Shaw, R. J. Shelly, Bill & Margo Smith, Kathy & Scott Sparrow, Jim Stewart, Chuck Uzzle, Scott Waite, Bill Waldron, Jay Watkins, Ethan Wells, Constance Whiston, Jacki Williams, Don Zimmerman.

I am very blessed to have such wonderful parents who are role models in my life. Fishing was a family activity while growing up, and I learned many valuable lessons about life, good friends, nature, ethical behavior, conservation, and courtesy to your fellow man from my Mom and Dad. I love you both very much.

Thanks also to my brothers, Stewart and William (Bill to the rest of the world), for allowing their kid brother to tag along on fishing trips, and to their families for graciously giving up one weekend a year for the annual Three Brothers Fishing Trip.

This book wouldn't have happened without the unselfish support and assistance of my family. Jake and Travis, you guys mean the world to me. Fishing trips wouldn't be nearly as fun without you.

Most importantly, I want to thank my best friend, Sally, for her support. We have been married for 21 years and have fished our way across the country. I couldn't imagine the last 21 years without her. All my love.

Index